No time for a

The ups and downs of life c

June Wolfe

For my wonderful Husband Clive who truly has the patience of a saint and my three amazing children who make me so proud
Also my parents Jan and Pete for their constant love and support.

No time for a siesta – *the ups and downs of life on a Spanish farm*

www.cortijoloslobos.com

Clive and June Wolfe live in a beautiful old Cortijo in the stunning countryside of Villanueva del Trabuco , Southern Spain, with their fifteen horses, two goats, one sheep, three dogs, seven cats, and ten chickens! They run a thriving holiday business – letting out their converted barns for self catering holidays, as well as providing horse riding, mountain biking, guided hikes and other excursions. Clive is a talented builder, working all week for clients and most weekends at home renovating the farm. June is kept busy looking after all the animals, home and family, the holiday business, taking clients riding, and through necessity has become a pretty competent builder herself! This is the story of their life now, and how it all began...........

Contents

-One-

Off to sunny Spain

It was in August 1999, whilst on holiday with my parents, Jan and Pete, at their holiday villa in Los Romanes, Southern Spain, that we made the impulsive decision that would change our lives for ever. My parents had decided to sell up in England and retire to Spain and were looking for a more suitable home to begin their new life. We had accompanied them on their house hunting trips and had fallen in love with an old farm, with land and fruit trees.

The estate agent typically quoted how much money could be made from harvesting the orchards - definitely to be taken with a pinch of salt! Though not gullible enough to believe everything we were told, it was enough to get us thinking. We started to dream about a simple life in rural Spain, living off the land, free of the stresses and strains of modern living and with a healthier environment for our three children to grow up in. It wasn't something we had even thought about until that fateful day, but suddenly it seemed like a wonderful idea. Since watching the TV series as a child in the seventies I had always had a secret yearning to live the self sufficient 'good life', and was never happier than when I was in jeans and wellies, helping out at the local riding stables. The change in lifestyle that I yearned for never seemed a possibility in England though, and I always pushed it to the back of my mind.

Clive's mum, Janet, had been living in the small white mountain village of Canillas de Aceituno for about eighteen years, so we were very familiar with this part of Spain. With both sets of parents living here it suddenly seemed the obvious thing to do – we would move here too!

Back at our home in Cambridgeshire we set about making our crazy dream come true. Our friends were quite shocked at our spur of the moment decision but they all went along with our plan – though many may have thought it, no one actually told us we were mad! Having put the house on the market, we soon had a buyer, though actually completing the sale did not prove to be so easy!

Folding up Clive's engineering business, selling cars and unwanted furniture and purchasing a left hand drive Land rover took over our lives in the following weeks.

We decided to employ a Spanish teacher to come to our home once a week for a couple of hours in an effort to at least achieve a small knowledge of Spanish to get us started. The plan was to concentrate more on the vocabulary that the children would need to get them off to a more confident start at school. The children loved their Friday afternoon lessons with Elda, their young and pretty Spanish teacher, she made learning fun, though poor Harry often struggled to stay awake enough to concentrate – being a naturally very lively child, he tended to burn himself out by the time it came to Friday, so it wasn't an ideal day for him. With a moving day target of Christmas, we didn't have time for many lessons, but we felt that anything was better than nothing. We did feel rather ashamed that in all the years spent holidaying in Spain we hadn't made the effort to pick up more of the language, but then at the time we could not have guessed where our future would take us.

The British Consulate did not seem to think that we needed to do anything special as regards sending our children to a Spanish school, merely suggesting that it would be a good idea to have their school records translated. The more we looked into the technicalities and legalities of moving to Spain, the more we realised that there was actually very little information available, and what was available was often conflicting. Being certain of the fact that we wanted to make a complete break, cutting off all ties with Britain and becoming legal residents in Spain, including paying into the Spanish system, we were determined to do everything properly. Little did we realise then how difficult that would always prove to be!

With a completion date of 16th December for our house sale, we set about arranging to transport our furniture, along with that of my parents, to their house in Spain.

The removal company assured us that it would take about a week from packing at our end to arriving at my parent's home. Clive had quite a large collection of

Bonsai trees which we decided would be fine on the lorry for that length of time, being a dormant period. We wanted the children to finish their last week at school and enjoy the exciting Christmas preparations and concerts, so our completion date was ideal. We had to agree to send the furniture a few days earlier however, as with Christmas coming up; this was all they could offer. The furniture was duly collected, but with one major problem – the removal company was now informing us that as it was Christmas, the furniture would not arrive in Spain until at least the end of the first week in January. Suddenly we had a real problem with the Bonsai trees – there was no way they could survive being stored in the dark without water for three weeks or more. Clive made the very reluctant decision to leave some of the trees with our friends and squeeze as many as we could into the caravan that we were towing down to Spain with us.

The transportation of our animals proved to be another problem. The injections and paperwork were complicated enough, but there is a strict time scale for having animals injected and flying them out – it has to be completed within a forty eight hour slot. With this in mind we had arranged to have our cat Simba inoculated on the morning of his flight. I had rung our local vet a couple of times during the previous week, to ensure that all would go as planned, but sure enough on the morning of the injections we arrived to find that they did not have them! There followed a very nervous few hours, waiting for the injections to be couriered from the Ministry of Agriculture, a two hour drive away. Thankfully they arrived just in time and we raced down to Heathrow with poor Simba crying all the way. Oscar, the African Grey Parrot was not so complicated and as it turned out, during the whole journey to Spain her paperwork wasn't even glanced at!

On 17th December 1999 we were on our way, after waving goodbye to all our friends, towing our caravan packed with Clive's precious bonsai trees, the kids and Oscar in the back of the car. We had not completed our house sale as planned, but with no furniture we decided to cut our losses and go anyway, trusting our solicitors to complete as soon as they could.

The journey through France and Spain was pretty uneventful, though sleeping in the Caravan at a service station in Northern Spain, with thick snow on the ground proved to be an adventure we hadn't contemplated!

Two days later we were winding our way up the mountain road to Canillas de Aceituno, and squeezing our caravan through the quaint narrow streets.

Finally we arrived at Sedella, where my parents were waiting to welcome us to their new home. We were here at last, starting our new life, with no house or job and barely two words of Spanish between us – were we mad?

Christmas was great, with all the family together and the feeling of anticipation for our life ahead. The Millennium eve was spent typically Spanish style in a freezing restaurant with our coats over our finery!

Spanish restaurants usually have lovely, cosy looking inglenook fireplaces, but for some reason rarely feel the need to light them. Contrary to the popular belief that it is always hot in Spain, the winters can actually feel colder than the uk, as the houses are designed to be cool in the summer, and are consequently very cold in the winter months, especially in the higher mountain villages. The lack of carpets, and curtains just adds to the bleakness. It was interesting to witness the New Year celebrations Spanish style - our introduction to the tradition of eating a grape for every chime of the clock at midnight had us in hysterics!

All too soon, the Christmas and New Year celebrations were over and real life had to begin. The children started school in Canillas, the first English children and welcomed with open arms. John, then twelve found it difficult to start with, being at a more self-conscious age, but Harry at eleven and Elizabeth being only nine, loved it and within two days all three were settled and happy and had made lots of friends. The teachers were fantastic and the kids picked up the language immediately and were soon inviting their new friends home to play. How proud I felt the first time I heard them talking to their friends in Spanish, as if the had been doing it all their lives. The length of the school day varied throughout the week, some days being morning only, and some a full day with school lunch in between. I was very glad that our children are not fussy eaters – their introduction to Spanish school food could have been quite traumatic, the menu usually consisting of oily stews full of beans and strange bits of meat – a slight problem for Elizabeth, who had been a vegetarian since the age of six. Despite the queen of Spain also being vegetarian, it is a concept that the Spanish find very hard to understand – their solution is usually to merely remove the offending meat from the dish and pass it back. Many is the time we have ordered something as simple as a tomato soup, thinking it a safe option, only to find pieces of jamon floating in it!

The process of enrolling the children in a Spanish school was easy – there seems to be very little official paperwork. We had their English school records and reports translated into Spanish before we came, but to be honest they didn't seem to be required and I doubt if they have even been looked at! Some people may have thought us cruel to throw our children in at the deep end and expect them to cope in a strange school in a different language but we believed, (and still do) that it was the best option. If we could have afforded to put them into an international school, they would not be bilingual as they are today. They were extremely lucky with their school in the Uk, which was very forward thinking and gave special lessons for bright children. Luckily for us, all three of the children had these extra lessons, which meant that when we brought them to Spain, their level of education was much higher than average. We felt that this gave them a cushion while getting to grips with learning Spanish, and it worked – the education system in Spain is different to the Uk – a child is held back to repeat a year if it fails to reach the required standard. Luckily, all three children managed to move up each year and leave school at sixteen, having passed their leaving certificates.

We did worry at first that the children were perhaps a little bit old to integrate easily into the Spanish system, but in hindsight at nine, eleven and twelve we think that they were an ideal age. They had the advantage of already having a good standard of English, both spoken and written which meant that we didn't have the added worry of teaching them their native language, but they were also young enough to pick up Spanish easily. Being the only English children in the school at the time made it much easier for them as they could only speak Spanish, whereas the English children that have joined the school since do not have the same advantage or incentive to speak Spanish – it is only natural to prefer to speak in your own language if you have the choice. Our children were very lucky, though they may not have thought so in the beginning! Strangely, they had the added advantage that, not having experienced foreign children before, some of the teachers didn't actually realise that they weren't Spanish and consequently made no allowances for them – very hard but ultimately the best thing that could have happened.

-Two-

Real life begins

Soon after moving to Spain, Clive started work building and landscaping for the local English community, and was very fortunate to be kept in constant work simply by word of mouth. His sympathetic renovations and artistic flair became very popular and he was thoroughly enjoying his new outdoor life, working for most of the year with his shirt off! Being an engineer by trade, and a very keen do- it -yourself enthusiast in the UK, his change of career came easy.

All that was left on our list was to buy a house! Clive's mum had seen a house whilst property hunting with a friend. It was in the campo, (countryside) outside a village called Villanueva del Trabuco, on the road to Zafarraya. We had never really been that way before, other than to pass by on the motorway to go to the Alhambra palace or skiing in the Sierra Nevadas. Driving up the winding mountain road that leads to Zafarraya, we entered another world. As we came out of Zafarraya and into the countryside approaching Trabuco the landscape was so different, so rocky and rugged, with wild flowers and oak trees. Then the land changed again, into olive groves and finally there was the farm house next to the biggest oak tree you've ever seen and with the most spectacular mountain view. We loved it the minute we stepped out of the car and onto the cobbled threshing circle. Inside, the house was everything we wanted, full of rustic charm, and with not too much work needed. The upstairs accommodation, previously used for grain storage was the icing on the cake. With the rustic beams, sloping roofs and quarry tiled floors, it was all we had dreamed of. In the corner was an enormous olive jar built into the wall and the grain storage bins, their sides topped with beautiful lengths of wooden beam, shining with the patina of decades of use were just stunning.

The many outbuildings with their cobbled floors and cane roofs were perfect for workshops and future renovations and the large flat field was an added bonus – a blank canvas for us to work on. It was all perfect for what we wanted to do. We all knew there and then that it was going to be our home. It reminded us of the highlands of Scotland, our favorite holiday destination in Britain. The children were so excited, making plans for our new life, with Elizabeth already planning where to put the first horse. What luck! The first house we'd viewed and we were in love!

The completion of our house in England finally happened on the tenth of January and with great relief we purchased our new home without any hiccups.

Signing the documents at the Notary was a true Spanish experience, with the chance to get to know our new neighbour, Jose Manuel, who had lived in our house as a child.

The furniture lorry also arrived that day. We were all so excited on the morning it was due, it felt like Christmas all over again. We had already started to forget what exactly we had packed and couldn't wait to start exploring the boxes. All did not go smoothly though. My parent's house was down a long bumpy dirt track and we were very worried that the lorry wouldn't make it. We needn't have worried on that score, as dirt tracks are a normal part of Spanish life and the lorry drivers are used to it, but the gate post to their very steep drive had to be demolished to enable the lorry to reverse in.

So began the seemingly endless task of transporting our belongings by small trailer the fifty kilometres from Sedella to our house in Trabuco – at least we became familiar with the many different routes we could take. We lost count of how many times we made that journey, but as we had decided not to move in until the children had their half term holiday at the end of February there was no real hurry, and moving our things in gradually meant that we had time to think about where to put things, and to clean first, which was a huge advantage.

Of course, we were all still living with my parents and it couldn't have been at a worse time. When we arrived they were in the middle of having central heating installed, but as is the norm with Spanish builders, the job had been left half done, with gaping holes in the walls for the pipe work. We were freezing and had to sleep in our ski thermals and wear gloves to read in bed!

To add to their problems, my poor parents had the worry of buying in water as they were not connected to the mains. With seven of us in the house, the water went down quickly and the situation soon became desperate. I lost count of the number of phone calls my mum made, trying to find a water transporter. Thankfully we did get some water in time but Oscar the parrot had obviously picked up on our problem, as to our amazement she started saying 'do you want some water?' a phrase she had picked up years ago, when my mother in law used to say it to her every time she filled her water dish – it was so funny, and good to laugh after all the tension.

March 1st 2000 saw us finally settled into our lovely farm house. Our new life had begun, not without its teething troubles and stresses, but easier than we could have imagined when we first took the gamble. Our romantic and idealistic idea before we got to Spain was to buy a ruin and live in the caravan, mortgage free, while we renovated, all the while living off the land and becoming self sufficient. While our new life had started on a relatively higher level, we knew that we had a long road ahead of us.

So began our tireless struggle to renovate, build, landscape and generally improve our new surroundings. Luckily the kids were picked up and dropped off by school bus right outside the door, which meant that I could get my scruffy clothes on first thing in the morning and work happily until dark, without interruption. Clive had to go to work, but once home, would carry on working. We were, and still are to a certain extent, workaholics, but we love it. We often had deadlines, if friends were coming to stay from England, which gave us the incentive to keep going (and a much welcomed holiday while they were here!)

About a month after we arrived we woke up one morning to find a very sad and bedraggled little dog, shivering in a stable. Clive at the time wasn't really a dog person and told us not to feed it, but gradually we won him over and we were allowed to keep Paja (Spanish for straw), so named, because we found her lying in a pile of straw. She was such a sweet dog and we all came to love her. Our menagerie had started. After that there were kittens, and lots more abandoned dogs – once word got around that we were English we became the unofficial pet dumping ground. Luckily most of them moved on of their own accord, but a few have stayed along the way.

Our next animal to arrive through choice was our first horse, Polly. A friend of Clive's mum happened to mention that she wanted to sell her horse to a good English home. Being horse lovers we just had to go and have a look, and of course we couldn't resist her. There was great excitement preparing for her arrival, cleaning out one of the barns and laying a new concrete floor, locating straw and feed. Our Spanish neighbours, Pedro, Remes and their daughter Gracia were a god send, they arranged everything for us. The day to collect her at last arrived but unfortunately the

Spanish man we had hired to transport her took his whip out and started whipping her to get her into the trailer which got her into such a state that there was no way she was going in! We were devastated, what were we going to do? We decided that the only way to get her home was to ride her, approx fifty kilometres from Sedella, through Alcaucin, Periana, Pulgarin, Alfarnetejo and finally over the top of our own mountain and home – what an adventure! John and I took turns to ride while the others followed in the car with food and water. Sometimes we removed her saddle and just walked her, Harry and Elizabeth taking it in turns to have a go at riding bare back. It took us ten hours, but it was an unforgettable experience. I had one tricky moment riding through a village called Periana. Just as we were overtaking a car the owner opened the door into the road and started to spray oil onto the hinges. As you can imagine, Polly was not impressed! Thankfully we survived that episode and the rest of the journey was uneventful.

As we finally arrived home, our neighbours and family were all there to meet us, not quite believing what we had done.

Polly was none the worst for her long walk and soon settled into her new life. She is quite a character and over the years, with our ever growing herd, has maintained her position as top mare.

-Three-

Polly makes her mark

It was thanks to Polly that we found out where the hospital was in Antequerra. On Johns thirteenth birthday he was putting her back in to her stable and she was being a bit naughty, not wanting to go in and leave the succulent grass she had been eating. Somehow, in her agitation she managed to kick John in the head. I heard a scream and saw John running towards me with what looked like a huge hole in his head and blood gushing out. Fortunately it looked much worse than it turned out to be and he only needed a few stitches, but thank goodness for our neighbours who took us to the hospital in their car. It soon became obvious that we needed a nice placid friend for Polly, not only for the company at home but also to give her confidence when out riding. We had started to wonder how on earth we had managed to ride her all those miles home that day, a case of ignorance is bliss I think! She was proving to be quite a difficult horse, not at all happy to be ridden out on her own; she either stopped and refused to move, or tried to gallop home. Luckily we managed to buy a lovely old horse called Carretta. She and Polly soon became great friends and going out for a ride became a pleasure rather than a chore.

Over the first few months in our new home we gradually came to grips with ticking off the never ending list of 'things to do' – residencias, (i.d. cards to prove that you are resident in Spain) paying into the social security system, re-registering our British plate car and obtaining Spanish driving licenses, as well as picking up Spanish, (easier when you have Spanish neighbours) and getting used to the Spanish way of life. How frustrating it was in the beginning, when we were in the middle of a particular building job and had run out of cement at two o'clock, to realise that we couldn't get any more until four thirty, or when we were rushing around on a morning shopping trip, trying to get everything done by two, so that we didn't have to kill time until the shops opened again at five. Of course it is second nature to us now but it took some getting used to, especially as we have never been able to adapt to the Spanish way of having siestas in the afternoon.

Our early days of working all day in the Spanish heat though, soon had us starting work on building a pool. Once again our neighbours came to the rescue. Conveniently for us, Jose Manuel works for the local builders merchants and was able to arrange a digger and delivery of all the necessary building materials. Unfortunately just days after the hole was dug we had torrential rain and we had a pool full of water quicker than we had imagined! Our first summer saw us sitting in the kid's paddling pool with our friends and Paja the dog, drinking gin and tonics. Polly lived in a stable by the house at the time with a courtyard that had a door into our courtyard. She was a very sociable horse and used to bang on the door for us to open it, so we had to erect a bar across for her to be able to see what was going on. She loved to stick her head in when we were eating outside and scrounge food (especially ice cream!) Obviously we did not make a habit of feeding her tidbits as horses do not take lightly to different food, but it was very entertaining. One day as we were leading her out of her stable for some grass she decided to stop and have a drink from the paddling pool. The trouble with Polly is that she also likes to splash her feet about in whatever container (or stream) she is drinking out of and before we could stop her she had ripped the bottom out of the pool. She does love water and has been known to try to roll in a stream when being ridden through it! The swimming pool was finally finished the following summer, with the whole family tiling it until dark every day to be ready in time for our next influx of friends.

During our first summer in Spain we had a holiday in England, as we had promised the kids that they could go back to see their friends. By then we didn't really want to go, but a promise is a promise and we set off on the long drive home, towing the caravan which we planned to stay in when we got there, (it was quite a novelty to be camping on the riverside park in our old home town of St. Neots in Cambridgeshire) and leaving Clive's mum Janet to house and animal sit. Poor Janet, while we were away she had quite an eventful time. On the very first day of her animal sitting duties, one of the horses dragged her off to a patch of grass, trapping her finger in the rope and nearly breaking it. Our next door neighbours came to the rescue again and after that Pedro put the horses out everyday and Remes supplied Janet with meals. To add to her problems, our lovely bread delivery man, Antonio, had been thoughtfully giving Janet stale bread to give to the horses, a common custom for all animals in Spain. Unfortunately Janet was unaware of the dangers of feeding horses dry bread and sadly poor old Carretta developed colic. Janet had to call a vet who told her that it was important that Carretta did not lie down. Janet didn't know what to do as she couldn't stay with Carretta all the time, but little Paja came to the rescue. Amazingly, every time Carretta lay down, Paja ran into the house and barked at Janet! What a clever little dog, she really was special.

Though it was good to see our friends, (and great for Clive to collect some of his long lost Bonsai trees) being in England only confirmed that Spain was now our home and we were very happy to get back.

Villanueva del Trabuco is a very friendly village, and enjoys its fiestas, of which there are many. From the Camping day in April, when the whole population heads for the campo to picnic and camp, then there is San Isidro in May, the Feria in June, again in August, then the big Fiesta in September which they celebrate in style, really getting into the spirit, with all the women in fiesta dresses and lots of horses. Of course Elizabeth and I had to join in and wear our dresses, very hot but guaranteed to make you feel part of the celebration. One year we rode the horses into town in our fiesta dresses to take part in the procession, great fun, especially galloping back home with our dresses flowing out behind us. Sadly, as the years have passed, we have felt less inclined to join in the horse activity, as the Spanish way of treating horses tends to conflict with our Natural Horsemanship beliefs.

In the September of our first year, we went to the horse fair in Velez Malaga and thanks to Elizabeth's ability to twist her granddad around her little finger, came home with a pretty black pony who we named Blackberry. The man we bought her from said he would deliver her and to our amazement she arrived in the back of a white van, barely higher than her, and she had a mule as a traveling partner! We were impressed that she had withstood the journey so well, she was so sweet and gentle when we unloaded her, and even tolerated us washing her down very thoroughly after we had discovered that she was infested with Bot flies. The next day was a different story though, and we soon came to realise that she had been drugged to keep her seemingly placid and calm. Poor Blackie turned out to be a very nervous, mixed up little horse and was responsible for kicking and biting quite a few people over the following few months, until we managed to convince her that she was safe with us and had no reason to be so bad tempered. Poor Clive had good reason to dislike Blacky in those early days – think of the worst possible place for a man to be kicked in, and you've guessed it – Blacky's aim was perfect. It was at the end of Elizabeth's tenth birthday party – all the guests were saying their goodbyes but Clive was nowhere to be seen. It later transpired that he had slunk off to bed quietly, in agony and embarrassment, not wanting to have to explain to anyone what had happened. Two days later he finally agreed to get himself checked out at the hospital – the two male doctors faces were a picture! Luckily, no serious harm was done and he has now forgiven Blacky, though I don't think he will ever quite trust her.

Now we had three horses, one each for the three children – we just needed two more. (Little did we know!)

On 12th October we have yet another local fiesta and each year until very recently it was celebrated two minutes up the road from us. The first year the boys decided to enter the horses in the Cintas competition. This consists of a length of rope strung high across a piece of ground between two posts, with tubes threaded over the rope, each one wrapped in a long length of ribbon with a ring at the end. The idea is to gallop your horse under the rope and spear the ring, which is no larger than a wedding ring, with a pencil or stick. If you are successful, the ribbon then unravels as you go. The boys did really well, and to our amazement Harry won on good old Carretta, getting four ribbons. They were the only children in the competition and some of the men didn't look too happy but it was great as it was Harry's twelfth birthday and he came home with a big silver cup. I almost had my own success in the mothers pig catching contest, but after giving a good chase and launching myself to the ground to catch the pig; it slipped away and was caught by someone else. Not to worry, we wouldn't have eaten it so it would have been just another pet to add to the menagerie.

Our first Christmas in Trabuco we decided that it would be a good idea to stage a traditional Christmas dinner early for our Spanish neighbours. I don't think they knew what had hit them! Pedro is always very reluctant to eat anything different and looked very suspiciously at everything we gave him. Always a sweet tooth, he did like the Christmas pudding though! Considering the amount the Spanish eat at weddings and first communions we were surprised that they seemed to be amazed at how much we ate! By now we felt like we had lived in Spain all our lives. The children were doing well at school and had lots of friends; we had a nice mix of Spanish and English friends and regular visits from all our old friends in England. Though often physically demanding and financially hand to mouth at times, life was good.

-Four-

The children grow up

A big advantage of moving here is the willingness of the children to travel on their own. That first summer when we went back to England for a holiday Elizabeth was not quite ten, but she decided that it would be a good idea if we left her in England to spend a bit longer with her friends and she would fly back to Spain on her own! At the time, Monarch airlines offered a free chaperone service for children, which was ideal. The three of them have regularly traveled back and forth to England on their own ever since. Moving to Spain has definitely given the children more freedom and independence – we never felt the same worry that we would have felt in England when they are out on their own. This is just as well, as the Spanish way of going out late and not coming home until the early hours would be very worrying otherwise!

Living in the campo is a bit difficult for teenagers. All three of the children had mopeds when they turned fourteen and studied for their moped licenses, which at least gave them a bit of independence, though they have been known to walk the five kilometers home in the summer after a Saturday night out. Of course there are a lot of plus points to life in the country– they have been able to run wild in a way that they would never have done in England. They also had a very close bond. If friends weren't available to play with, they had each other, and we never heard the cry of 'I'm bored' that is so common among children. Being very outdoor, sporty children they were in their element, with mountains to climb, horses to ride, mountain bikes, skiing and swimming, they were never short of things to keep them occupied. My parents were also a big influence in their lives at that time – the children would often going skiing with Grandad, and were all introduced to the joys of Scuba diving , one of my parents main hobbies. It was great that though they now lived in Spain, they still enjoyed the benefits of living near their Grandparents and being able to share their lives with them, all the many birthday parties and outings, nothing had changed in that respect, my parents had seen our children almost every day since they were born, and it was a huge bonus that they could still get to see each other regularly.

During our first year here I was feeling really smug, with my lovely healthy 'outdoor' children, who also devoured books by the dozen in their spare time. That is, until my parents very kindly decided to buy them Satellite television as a reward for doing so well at school – oh dear, soon they were more like normal teenagers!

Of course the internet has not helped either, though I would not be able to run the business without it so I can't complain. The slow dial up system that we had in the early days was so frustrating at times but we were lucky to have it at all, at a time when a lot of our local friends struggled to have even a telephone installed.

Teenagers do have a habit of comparing their lives with their friends, and of course over the years we have had to contend with Spain being blamed for anything wrong in their lives, i.e. The internet is better in England, you don't get so much home work, sixth form is so cool – and so on. Of course the constant succession of their friends that visited from the UK thought otherwise and reveled in the freedom they had when they were here, returning year after year – we have such fond memories of those carefree summers, with gangs of children and teenagers messing about in the pool.

Our eldest, John, did find out for himself where his home really was when he went back to England at sixteen to attend an army college in Harrogate. Having passed Spanish school and achieving his Titulo (leaving certificate) after only three years here we were very proud of him. He decided that he wanted to make his career in the British army, being such a fitness fanatic and also very disciplined and tidy. He set off in September 2003 to start his new life and found the army life everything he had expected – he loved it and thrived in the environment, enjoying the many academic and travel opportunities that came with it. He has great memories of a trip they did to northern Spain where his translation skills were put to good use, and the Spanish lads he met there said he had an accent just like their friends from Malaga! Surprisingly, academically John found he was advanced compared to most of the English lads. Having studied in a foreign language since the age of twelve he fully expected to be behind the English curriculum but that was not the case. Expats with school age children may naturally have concerns about the standard of education in the Spanish schools, so it is nice to know that they must be getting something right.

John's problems with his army life began when they were allowed to go home for the weekend. Of course it was impossible for John, and he started to realise that this could become a problem. As time went on, it also occurred to him that when he went away on tour of duty, where ever he was in the world he would always be sent back to England and only then would he be able to find his own way back to Spain. He started to become home sick, missing his life in Spain and hating England. Eventually, having stuck it out for fourteen months he decided to leave and happily for us, came home, especially as it was just a month before he was due to set off for Iraq. It was lovely for us to know that he had discovered for himself that actually it was better here and that Spain was his home. At still only eighteen, John had not lost anything and had experienced so much, he didn't regret his time in the army and he says that all boys should do it. On his return to Spain he started college in Antequerra, along with his younger brother Harry and some of his Spanish friends. He finished college in 2007 and started work for a computer company on the coast. At the same time he set up home with his girlfriend Rebecca, who had moved out from England to attend a hairdressing college. John and Rebecca originally met when they were just two years old, at playschool in England, and went through school together until John left to move to Spain. Rebecca was the best friend of the daughter of friends of ours from England, who all came out to visit every single year. When the girls were sixteen they wanted their first holiday without their parents and came out to stay in our guest cottage. I had suggested to their parents that it would be a good idea, as they would have their independence but we would be on hand should they have any problems. John and Rebecca got together, but split up when John joined the army. They met up again when Rebecca came to the coast on holiday with a friend, and have been together ever since. In August 2007 they got married here in Spain, at a local hotel. It was made extra special by the fact that our neighbor, Gracia, who was twenty two when we moved here and like an older sister to the children, is the local Justice of the Peace and was able to carry out the ceremony. It was a perfect day, with all our family and friends flying over for the event, and the evening reception held here at the farm, with dancing on the pool patio. The wedding took place in the morning, outside, American style, in the shade of the hotel, followed by a sit down lunch in the hotel dining room. Then it was time for Clive and I to rush home to frantically prepare the evening reception, for over one hundred guests. Thank goodness for the help of our friends who hadn't been able to attend the actual wedding and were still behind at the farm - without us even asking, they had rallied together, even the children's teenage friends all chipped in and we arrived back to find the horses fed, tables set in the courtyard, most of the work done for us, all we had to do was prepare the food for the evening, though there was barely time to draw breath before the first guests arrived.

Sadly for us, Rebecca found she missed her Mum too much, and on discovering soon after the wedding that she was pregnant, they took the decision to move back to England. Of course we miss John terribly, and are surprised that after his army experiences and being adamant that his home was in Spain he has gone back but we hope he has a happy life there. He now lives in our old home town, so at least has lots of friends and family around him. In May two thousand and nine they had their little girl, Myah, and in July 2011 their son, Sebastian was born. Of course with all of our commitments here, it is incredibly difficult for us to get away, which makes visiting almost impossible – sadly for us we will never get to be the 'hands' on Grandparents we would like to be.

Harry finished college in 2008 and while looking for work here in Spain, saw an appeal on English television for young people wishing to work on the Super Yachts, owned by the mega rich such as film and sports stars. The recruitment process was huge, with over five hundred original applicants. He and Elizabeth both applied and got through to the final hundred. After passing a succession of interviews

Harry finally achieved a place, one of only twenty five, to train as an engineer. Since within the twenty five places offered, for a mix of Deckhands, Stewards and Engineers only three were for Engineer positions, he had done extremely well. After an intensive three week, all expenses paid course in Plymouth at the naval yard, he was due to get a placement immediately on board a yacht, be given a six month contract with a great salary, and sail off to the Caribbean, lucky thing!

We had proudly waved him off, not expecting to see him again for months, but sadly, as with many businesses in the recession, it seems that even that industry is suffering, and he eventually was told that there were not going to be any jobs. What a waste of all that training – it certainly didn't come cheap. I suppose he can at least be grateful to have all of the qualifications he achieved whilst there, such as fire fighting and deep sea rescue and of course it was a great experience, but such a shame that it didn't end in a job. After trying for several months to find something in that field, Harry finally settled for a job on the coast in a shop. At least he was earning money and was able to move into his own flat and run a car, so we were grateful for that, but not quite the career he had anticipated. Still, Harry being Harry, we knew that he wouldn't waste too much time doing something he wasn't happy with. He is now training to work in the airline industry, starting at the bottom, but hoping to move into engineering in the future, in these difficult times it is at least a step in the right direction.

Elizabeth, at eighteen, had qualified as a veterinary nurse and had been doing work experience at a veterinary practice in Antequerra. As a younger girl she wanted to make her career with horses. She had big ambitions to study in California with Monty Roberts (the famous horse whisperer) but had since had lots of other ideas, including training to be a Scuba diving or skiing instructor, just two of her many hobbies. After completing college, while still looking for a job, she was a great asset, practicing her skills on our own horses, and demonstrating 'join up' to any of our clients that were interested.

From an early age she has been interested in Monty's work and developed her skills by reading his books. A few years ago we attended a course with a local woman who trained with Monty Roberts and runs a natural horsemanship centre in Bobadilla. We also built a round pen and now Elizabeth has all the tools she needs to practice, including plenty of young horses. Elizabeth has a natural affinity with all animals, especially horses, and has backed and trained some of our young horses single handedly. To her credit these horses have become our riding client's favorites to ride.

In February two thousand and nine, after trying unsuccessfully to get a job as a veterinary nurse, she left home to become a Nanny for a family in Germany. With Spain being in such a deep recession, and jobs impossible to find, she felt that she may as well be doing something useful, and see a bit more of the world. She wanted to learn German, as at the time she was still thinking about a job in the veterinary profession and here in Spain, it is the British and the Germans (as well as the Spanish of course) who use the vets on the coast, and she felt that being able to speak German would improve her chances of obtaining a job in the future. We were very proud of our confident and independent daughter and though obviously nervous, as parents, of letting her go at such a young age, knew that she would be fine – she was so mature for her age. We were slightly concerned about how she would cope, bearing in mind that she had no experience with children, but we needn't have worried, she soon found that children were not much different to horses and other animals, you just had to learn to speak their language! Her first Facebook comment on arrival did make us laugh though – "Elizabeth thinks baby poo stinks!" Good old Facebook, despite thinking of it as something that only the children used, and not for us 'oldies' I have to admit to finding it a precious tool for keeping in touch with the children, and also family and friends. I have now got so many old friends and family members back in my life, that I am sure I would probably never have seen again, and it also helps with the business, with quite a few holidays sold purely because of Facebook connections (and the fabulous photo albums that you can make public!) Elizabeth, or Lily as she was more frequently becoming known as, soon settled very happily into her life in Hamburg.

The family she was working for loved her and she was making lots of new friends. She had also started scuba diving again, having 'hit it off' with the owner of a dive shop, who later agreed, after learning of her ambition to become a scuba diving instructor, to help her through her exams, allowing her to work for him on Saturday mornings to pay towards the costs. After working as a Nanny for a year, she decided to leave and move into her own flat, nearer to the city and soon found herself a couple of part time jobs, to help fund her diving. Typically, for Lily, the family that she used to Nanny for missed her so much that they invited her to move back in with them, rent free. They had already employed another Nanny to replace Lily, so didn't need her to work for them any more, but just wanted to have her living there again. She did move back for a while, it seemed silly not to, as she was trying to save money, but found it too difficult, living further from the city and eventually moved back out, though she still maintains contact with them and sees them on the children's birthdays and other family occasions.

-Five-

Tragic times

Our life here in Spain has not always been a bed of roses, we have had our fair share of tragedies and disasters along the way.

A year after her arrival our lovely little dog Paja was killed on the road outside our house.

That morning I had found Paja asleep on Lily's bed, and told her off, saying she knew she wasn't allowed on the bed (though I am sure that Lily often let her), and shooing her into the kitchen. A little while later I went out to collect the bread from the bread delivery man, who told me that my dog had been run over, just down the road outside Jose Manuels house. With my heart in my mouth I ran, not wanting to believe what I could see, and desperately hoping that she would just be injured. Sadly, she was dead, though it was obvious from her injuries that she hadn't suffered, it would have been very quick. Poor Paja, she had never been a very healthy little dog, we think the reason she was dumped on us was because of the ulcers she used to get on her teats, and she always lacked energy, though she was so loving and loyal. The trouble was, she liked to lie on the warm tarmac, and unfortunately this day, she ran out of luck.

When it happened I ran next door to Remes and Gracia in tears and was given a cup of chamomile tea to calm me. Remes helped me pick poor Paja off the road and we buried her in the garden. I was upset for weeks afterwards, actually crying myself to sleep at times, I couldn't believe how much I missed her funny little face and character. Her absence also left a huge hole in my life, I had lost my little friend, my companion when the kids were at school and Clive was at work.

Soon after Paja's death, Clive had a head on collision with a lorry and wrote our Landrover off. It was not his lucky day – he had set off to do a job an hour away, but having got there, it was pouring with rain, and he had no option but to turn round and drive all the way home. It was on the last stretch, five minutes before the house that the accident happened. To make matters worse, I was laying on the sofa in my dressing gown, suffering from Flu, when he phoned to ask me to come and pick him up in our other car. I can remember my feelings of desolation, standing in my dressing gown in the pouring rain, gazing at our lovely car, now only fit for the scrap yard. The problem with our roads is that they are narrow and windy, and not suitable for the large lorries that sometimes sneak through, on route to the quarries. If you meet one on a bend on a wet day, there is not much room for error. Luckily Clive was not hurt, and we were able to find a replacement Landrover in our village, which was a huge relief as without it Clive could not continue his building work.

Then came our worst disaster of all - our house caught fire, after we had very stupidly gone out and left a fire burning in the hearth. John had been home from the army for a few days, and we had decided to leave early to take him back to the airport, spending a bit of quality time with him first, and having some lunch in Malaga. Ironically, we had just been killing time really, and could have come home much earlier. I had also had that feeling, as you often do, soon after setting off that morning, that I had forgotten to do something. It's so easy to regret not turning back and checking, but hindsight is a wonderful thing. As we pulled up on the threshing circle, I could see thick black smoke bellowing out of our chimney, and I knew straight away that something was seriously wrong. With sinking hearts we unlocked the kitchen door, to find the house full of smoke and an armchair and wall by the fire still smoldering. Our lovely parrot, Oscar, was dead at the bottom of her cage but incredibly, all our other animals were outside in the courtyard– an amazing piece of luck as in the cold weather they are normally snuggled up indoors. We comfort ourselves in the fact that poor Oscar wouldn't have suffered, with birds being so sensitive to smoke, but it is a terrible loss, as she had been part of our family for about fifteen years, since we were given her by Clive's mum, when she herself moved to Spain. Janet had rescued her from a pet shop in the Isle of Man as she looked so sad and had a broken wing and no feathers. Oscar said hundreds of words, all in our voices; she was just like a little person. I had never been happy about her boring little life, though, and have tried to convince myself that she is better off dead as she could have lived in her little prison for another fifty years! She was stuck in her cage, day after day, with only the rare taste of freedom if Clive or one of the boys had time to let her out. She loved to stand on their shoulders and snuggle up to their face, or feed their fingers as if they were her babies. She hated women though and though I was the one that fed her and cleaned her out I got no thanks for it and she loved to peck my fingers (while at the same time saying 'ooh! you bugger' in Janet's voice!). Poor little Pheobe, Lily's ferret, had a very narrow escape, as she had been in Lily's bedroom, but luckily the smoke had not gone under the door or we would have been mourning two beloved pets.

The house was a terrible mess after the fire; the smoke had even got inside the fridge. Nothing was spared and the clean up operation was huge. Our friends and family were amazing though and helped for days on end with the cleaning and re-decorating. The Spanish insurance company was not so helpful though; we eventually had to settle for a payout of only about half of our loss. They are very clever – knowing that we desperately needed the money to pay for the repairs, they offered to settle quickly for much less money, or told us we could pursue more, but it could take years! Needless to say, we have now changed insurance companies and use a fire guard! Life carries on. A few months after Paja died I persuaded Clive to let me get another rescue dog, so we got Scruffy – a worthy replacement. I had asked my Vet if he knew of any dogs needing a home, specifying that I would really like a water dog, like Paja. Scruffy does have a wool coat that can look like an old sheepskin rug, complete with dreadlocks, when he is in need of a trim, but that is where the resemblance ends, and though he does like to paddle in streams, he hates to swim. He is a lovely dog, and a firm favorite with our guests, who often send him e-mails. He even has his own Facebook Fan page. He spends most of the summer sharing himself between the guest cottages, probably depending on which lot of guests are doing the tastiest bbq, and has even been known to have 'sleepovers'. We recently received an email from guests, thanking us for a wonderful holiday, and reminding us that "Scruffy likes to have a sausage at nine pm"

Soon after giving Scruffy a home, little Suzy was dumped outside our house, skin and bone and a shivering wreck. The children found her one winter morning, quivering on a pile of leaves by the gate. Clive refused to keep her, saying he didn't want any more dogs, but she was such a sad little thing, we just had to feed her, and the children soon smuggled her into an old kennel that had been built by the previous owners. Obviously Clive was fully aware of what we were doing, but persisted in saying 'I hope you're not feeding that dog' every time he saw it.

 Poor little Suzy, she was so desperate for love, we think she was a hunting dog that perhaps was abandoned because she was no good, as she is terrified of guns and bangs and even if you swat a fly on the wall, she runs and hides. Thunderstorms traumatise her completely, and she occasionally has epileptic fits which are very unpleasant to witness but I am assured by the vet are not a problem, though in later years it did cause problems with the other dogs for a time.

Normally, the dogs all got on very well, but to my dismay soon after Suzy developed epilepsy something happened that made my blood run cold. I was in the kitchen when I heard the dogs barking. It just sounded like they were playing so I ignored it, but then I heard a pitiful crying sound, and on running out, discovered that Chici (our neighbours dog at the time) and Scruffy were attacking Suzy, who was having a fit. Luckily she was fine, but I dread to think what would have happened if I had not been there. It is very worrying and upsetting to realise that even the friendliest dogs can revert to their natural instincts when another animal is perceived as a victim.

Suzy is a funny little character and likes to be carried like a baby. She can also do a brilliant Meerkat impression; it is now her party piece! She gets very jealous if I give any other animal attention as she sees herself very much as my dog, but she is very kind with smaller animals and will allow the cats and kittens to play with her and groom her and she has even been known to suckle our kittens and baby goat (another story!). When Suzy first arrived we already had a second dog, a young female dog, Jess. Our Spanish neighbours had a beautiful black Spaniel, Nora, the sweetest, kindest dog you have ever met. She had a litter of puppies just before Lily's eleventh birthday. It was normal for Nora to have at least one litter of puppies each year, and sadly, as is the norm in Spain, when the puppies were born they were usually disposed of in a sack; it was actually thought more humane to allow dogs to continually have puppies, than to have them sterilised. This particular time, Lily had witnessed Remes using some metal tongs to remove each puppy from the kennel and place it in the sack, as she couldn't bear to touch them, she said they looked like rats. Lily was so horrified, that she took over, and did the dreadful deed herself, feeling that it was somehow 'kinder' to put them in the sack by hand. Having heard what was happening, we agreed to let Lily keep one of the puppies, who she named Jess. Our neighbours also decided to keep one, which they named Chici. Anyway, Jess was due to be spayed but as the time for her operation drew closer, we had noticed that neighborhood dogs had been taking a keen interest in Suzy, and were worried that she could be pregnant. I persuaded Clive that even though he didn't want to keep Suzy, it would be sensible to take her to be fixed at the same time, and off we went. The day of the operation was very cold, and when I arrived to collect the two dogs, the vet made a big fuss of finding some old jumpers to keep the dogs warm in the car.   He stressed that it was important for them to be kept indoors in the warm. You can just imagine Suzy's smug little smile of satisfaction, the minute she finally made it over the threshold and into the house – I don't think the smile has left her face since. Now she reigns like the queen of Sheba, sitting on her favourite armchair in front of the fire. I'm sure she smirks at Clive whenever she looks at him, poor Clive, he never stood a chance. That Christmas, Lily also gained the pet she had wanted since a tiny child. My parents had spotted a ferret for sale in their local pet shop, and asked us if it was ok for them to give it to Lily for Christmas. Of course we couldn't say no and little Phoebe, an albino Ferret, became the best Christmas present ever. Ferrets aren't to be taken on lightly, unless you merely want to keep them in hutches outside for hunting. To keep a ferret as a family pet requires a lot more dedication than at first appears. We soon found out that you cannot keep a female ferret unless you either have it sterilized, or allow it to continually have litters of young. Apparently ferrets go into a decline and die if not allowed to breed. Luckily we found this out in time, and took Phoebe to have her sterilised. She was such a tiny little ferret though that when we arrived at the vets, we were told that it would not be possible to operate. Luckily, the vet agreed to go ahead, and Phoebe was fine.

She had the sweetest nature, and never bit anyone her whole life. She lived loose in Lily's bedroom like a cat, with a litter tray, sleeping in a drawer, in a little sleeping bag that my mum made especially for her. Ferrets are renowned for their unpleasant smell, but if kept indoors, and clean, their smell is quite mild, musky but not intolerable, though the friends that often shared Lily's room may not have entirely agreed. We are probably all familiar with the expression 'ferreting around', but I must admit that until we owned a ferret, I hadn't given much thought to the meaning. Ferrets do actually 'ferret around'. They love to scuttle around, stealing things and hiding them, Lily could never find a rubber when she was trying to do her homework. She also had to hang a spare quilt cover down from her high cabin bed so that Phoebe could climb up and get in bed with her. If she didn't do this, Phoebe would trash her bedroom at five am to get attention, just like a naughty toddler! (and yes – Ferrets do actually run up your trouser legs!)

Cats were also a big part of our growing menagerie. As well as Simba, our big English ginger tom, we gained Rambo, as a little ginger kitten. He lived up to his name as he was very sweet and loving and licked your nose – before taking a chunk out of it! Another of our earlier cats was Buffy (as in the vampire slayer) who came to us one Halloween (hence the name). I was out riding when this tiny little tabby kitten, no more than eight weeks old, started following me. When I arrived home, approximately two miles later, she was still with me so of course she had to stay. Even now, years later, she prefers to live with the horses, snuggled up in the stables, only venturing up to the house in the winter when she gets cold. After Buffy, over the years, we enjoyed a succession of different cats, some abandoned in our rubbish bin at the front of the house, some rescued from friends who could no longer keep them. Sadly, some of them do not stay for long, either wandering off, never to be seen again, or getting run over (always after we have paid to have them sterilised of course!)

-Six -

Chicken trouble

We were very keen from the start to have free range hens, so once we had sorted out suitable night time accommodation for them they duly arrived. Scruffy thought Christmas had come early and couldn't understand why he wasn't allowed to chase them. We also discovered that he could get through the hole into the chicken shed. Luckily we soon taught him that he wasn't allowed and we haven't had a problem with him since. Our other big worry was remembering to shut them in at night and sadly one night we forgot with tragic consequences – we woke up in the morning to find them all dead and scattered around the field – clearly a fox had been to visit. It was very upsetting.

We quickly replaced them but we always have the worry that one day we will forget again – we need to invent a door that automatically closes at night. We make do with an alarm on our mobile phone, which leads to a chorus of 'chicken alarm' when it goes off – quite funny if we are not at home at the time! If we are going out for the evening and know that we are going to be home after dark, we make an amusing sight, clapping and calling, trying to round the hens up into their house, and of course there is always one that refuses to play the game. During the day they run free, wreaking havoc on my precious garden, but looking so comical that I could never bring myself to fence them in. One of these days when I'm digging over the garden I am going to accidentally chop one of their heads off as they are always pecking the freshly dug soil for worms.

The only other worry we have had with them is chicks – that is definitely a learning curve. It was exciting the first time we realised that we had a broody hen, but we quickly discovered that every time a new egg was laid she gathered it into her collection and soon had too many. We decided to put a cross on the eggs she had already and remove any subsequent ones – not as easy as it sounds. I am ashamed to admit that we did serve up a half boiled chick for breakfast! We learned by our mistakes and the next time we had a broody hen we separated her until the chicks hatched and were big enough to go in with the others. The worrying doesn't stop there though, as you then have to decide when they are big enough to go out. One year when the chicks were running around outside two eagles started circling overhead. Luckily I was outside with them at the time and was able to protect them but it was quite upsetting.

One of the hens got caught in a stampede in the horses field and just curled up under her wings and gave up. When I rescued her she had a broken leg but apart from that was fine. Our friend Sue is a nurse so she came round to have a look and we put a splint on the leg, not really feeling very hopeful. I kept her in a stable for three weeks and after that she was fine, she didn't even have a limp. It wasn't too easy at first to introduce her back to the other hens though – now I understand where the expression 'hen pecked' comes from – hens can be really evil to one of their own, if they sense that there is something wrong. That poor little hen, I had to introduce her slowly, day by day, letting her be with the others while I was there to watch over her, and gradually increasing the time, until they accepted her back. Hens can also be very unpleasant to the cockerel too, one poor cockerel we introduced had to put up with having his feet pecked until they bled for his first few days, until he had asserted himself and gained their respect.

Christmas of two thousand and four found us taking on perhaps our most difficult new addition – a new born baby goat! Holly, as we named her, was rescued from a local farm as she had failed to suckle and the farmer had left her to die. I was asked if I would have her and like a fool said yes. She was a tiny little scrap, and could barely drink. I had to force her to take one ounce at a time from a baby's bottle. She just about stayed alive though, surviving pneumonia over Christmas, despite the vet telling me that she would die, and to my relief gradually becoming stronger and drinking more. She thought she was my baby and had to be cuddled to sleep on my lap and followed me around calling muuuum, muuum. She slept in front of the fire with Suzy and Buffy – all curled up together, and tried to suckle from Suzy, who very bravely tolerated it! Eventually she turned the corner and got stronger every day, soon guzzling down a whole bottle of milk in minutes. Just when we thought her problems were over she managed to get trampled by one of the horses, having followed me down to the field. Luckily she survived with just a bad limp, so off I went to the vet to find out if anything was broken. The vet could not believe that she was doing an x-ray on a goat! There were no bones broken but she came home with a full leg bandage. I certainly got some funny looks, carrying a goat with a bandaged leg through the streets of Antequerra. Of course, once her leg was better and she became livelier it was obvious that her life living in the kitchen would have to stop – but how? She was becoming a menace and could jump up onto the table if anyone left a chair out. The day I caught her jumping the sofa, while at the same time spraying out a trail of little pellets of poo was the last straw – enough was enough! The problem was that she thought she was half human, half dog and did not take lightly to being put in a stable. The fact that a goat should never live alone was another problem – only one solution – we had to get another goat. We soon acquired Fudge and now they are the best of friends and have been living happily outside for years now.

We seem to be destined to rescue birds too. Our most interesting was a Little owl that was on the road outside the house. It most likely had been knocked slightly by a car as it was not hurt but was in shock. We kept it in a cat box over night and fed it worms which it loved, and then luckily it was able to fly away the next day. Our most exciting owl experience happened one beautiful balmy summer night, when we were enjoying a drink outside in our courtyard. The air was so still and the stars were amazingly bright, it was totally magical. Suddenly, we heard an incredible beating of wings, you could almost feel the draught, and then swooping right over our heads came an Eagle owl. It was so magnificent; it almost brought tears to my eyes, a truly unforgettable experience. We have since been lucky enough to see one perched on top of an old electricity pylon by the road, but nothing quite as exciting as that night. Less interesting are the pigeons that we seem destined to rescue – we have now had two, one with a broken wing and one a broken leg. They lived in the tack room, pooing everywhere, until they had mended and could fly away. Buffy would hang around outside the door ever hopeful that I would let her in!

On a bigger scale, we started collecting and rescuing horses. Unfortunately rescuing still meant paying for them, but when you have seen a horse in a sad situation it is hard to walk away. With Polly, Carretta and Blackie already, we did hope that one day we would have a couple more so that the whole family could ride together. Sadly, Carretta died a year after we bought her from a tumor on her kidney. She had got very thin and had lost her appetite. I had tried several local vets, but no one seemed to know what was wrong with her. It got to the point where even if we picked succulent hedgerow grass for her she wasn't tempted to eat. I finally found a lovely English vet on the coast, who agreed to come and see her.

After spending over an hour examining her thoroughly, and talking about various tests she could do, she did an internal examination and found the tumor – the size of a football. There was no other option, we had her put to sleep, all of us having a last cuddle, and our final memories are of her standing amidst a blanket of poppies, by the horse's field. At that time, all those years ago, we were unaware of any laws regarding disposal of livestock, and our neighbor simply called a man with a digger and we buried her right where she fell, in the garden. We now have a lovely old olive tree, especially bought to mark her grave and a large standing stone that we found near the river makes an impressive gravestone. I only wish that we could dispose of all of our horses in such a sympathetic manner, when their time comes, but sadly we now have to call the Ministry of Agriculture to send a lorry – something I am dreading.

We replaced Carretta with Lucy (Andalusia), a very pretty and gentle mare who was pregnant when we bought her, though we had no idea when the foal was due. Typically, she had her foal in the early hours of the morning and when we went in to feed her, there he was, already standing up and suckling – what an amazing sight. His birthday was such a happy day, with our neighbours and family coming to visit the new born. Lucy was a natural mum and seemed quite happy to show him off. She remains an incredible mum – the cheeky Leo, at nearly four still suckled from her occasionally; we wanted her to wean him naturally but she seemed to have other ideas! Even now, aged nine, he calls for her whenever she is out riding without him.

Our first rescue horse was Morena, a little bay horse who had been left in a field without enough food. Lily's best friend at the time, Celeste, wanted to have her own horse and keep it at ours, so we had started looking out for the ideal horse. Once we had seen Morena we couldn't leave her, but unfortunately Celeste's step dad didn't like her, so we ended up keeping her ourselves. She is a funny little character and to this day is possessive over her food, making a noise like a dinosaur if another horse goes to close. She was a great favourite with children, so trustworthy, but she would also do a very slow little canter when the rest of the horses were trotting and was perfect for teaching children. She is now incredibly old and frail. We will never know her true age as her paperwork was false, but she has been retired now for many years and every winter I think it will be her last, though so far, she has refused to go. Last winter I really thought we were losing her, I even got as far as phoning the vet to ask about having her put to sleep. She would lie down on her bed at night, and in the morning we couldn't get her up again. It was so upsetting, we literally had to haul her up and walk her around, and then she seemed to ease up and be ok. This went on for a couple of days and just when I had decided that enough was enough, she suddenly rallied, and was fine again. I know that we can't have her for much longer, but I am dreading the day it happens.

Next we bought Bracken, a Shetland pony. She is ideal for small children to ride and is a cheeky little thing. She is an amazing escape artist and often gets out of the field. One day she disappeared. We suddenly heard a neigh and found her in the pool pump house – she had gone in and somehow closed the door behind her! We have had to put a padlock on the feed room and keep it locked – if you just loop the padlock through she can get it out and open the bolt! One morning I went down to find the horses having a party in the feed room – Bracken had opened the door! What a mess – there was poo everywhere and most of the food had either been eaten or spilt on the floor. We make sure we keep the door padlocked at all times now! I have lost count of the times that she has almost locked me in the chicken shed, which happens to share the oldies paddock, where Bracken lives – it has a bolt on the outside, but nothing on the inside, so if she ever succeeds I will be stuck in there – I try to have my mobile phone in my pocket at all times! She did shut Clive in once, but luckily I was nearby and he was able to call out to me. Bracken has formed a strong bond with another of our old horses, Alfie, and the two cant bear to be separated, it is so sweet, though I think also very clever of Bracken, who though a relatively young pony, now lords it up with the two old rescue horses and gets to pinch all their food!

What with the pigeons and the horses our poor tack room was destined to be a mess, though now that we have built a smart new one outside of the horses paddock it tends to stay a lot neater. Another problem we have to deal with is mice. If left to their own devices they can be very destructive. Sadly we have to resort to putting poison down which I hate as I actually find mice very appealing. Ironically I will go to great lengths to save them if I find them drowning in water buckets. Once I rescued one poor mouse that had almost drowned and put him up on top of some straw bales to dry in the sun. In the blink of an eye Buffy was there and before I could stop her had knocked the mouse to the ground, where one of the hens promptly speared it with its beak! (if you knew what went into your free range eggs they might not seem so good!) That poor mouse just wasn't meant to live!

-Seven-

The rescue centre grows

When you buy a horse in Spain they come with a green card. This card is issued when the horse is a year old and each time the horse goes on to a new owner the card has to be updated with the new details. In typically Spanish fashion this involves a trip to the ministry of agriculture in Antequera with the previous owner and identity cards, to have the new information transferred. We have also had to register as a zoo! (Probably not too far from the truth in our case!) Apparently if you own more than five horses this is compulsory, and involves a lot of paperwork, microchips, vet inspections and other red tape. It baffles me how when I am out riding I still see so many poor horses, stuck in tiny stables, often never seeing the light of day, this new legislation doesn't seem to apply to them!

It seemed we were destined to rescue horses. Alfie, our next horse, was owned by an English family who admitted that they didn't know anything about horses and had luckily realised it before it was too late. When she arrived she was incredibly fat and could hardly walk as she had chronic laminitis, a very painful illness affecting the feet. We thought she would just be a companion for Leo when we took the others out riding, but once we had slimmed her down she became a lovely horse to ride. She is in her late twenties now and retired. The evidence of her hard life is there to see; she has grey rings of hair round her front feet from scarring caused by being hobbled, and grey scars on her nose from the harsh Spanish bridle she has worn most of her life. She is a bit of a bad tempered old mare, but I feel that given her history she has a right to be. She did manage to have two foals by Leo and she has a close bond with both as well as Bracken the Shetland pony, and tolerates the company of Morena, her other field companion. Alfie's first foal, Spirit, was a bit of a surprise. Leo was only a year old the previous summer, and we hadn't expected him to be fertile; we have since found out that though it is not usual before eighteen months, horses can be fertile from one year! With Leo being such a mummy's boy, and continuing to suckle milk until he was four, it was even more unexpected — talk about having your cake and eating it!

The problem with having a horse castrated in Spain is the flies. It is important with an operation that leaves an open wound that it is done at a time of year when there aren't many flies, but also when it is warm enough for the horse to stay outside after the operation so that he can move around and keeps the circulation going to reduce swelling. This leaves spring or autumn, but unfortunately every time we decided to have the operation done the weather would get bad, and then before we knew it the flies were upon us. This resulted in Leo not having his operation until he was nearly three. From a behavioral point of view this was not a problem, as he has always been a lovely natured horse, but on the foal front it was a disaster. (Though of course we don't think so now.)

Anyway, unbeknown to us Alfie became pregnant. It wasn't until the early summer of two thousand and four that we started to be suspicious. Alfie had become a bit thin over the winter and we had been slowly fattening her up – a difficult process for horses prone to Laminitis. Consequently it was no surprise that she was getting fatter, but all of a sudden she seemed to look very fat and we decided that we needed to ring the vet to find out one way or another. It was a few more weeks before the vet could come, but we finally got the pregnancy confirmed. The vet said that she still had a few months to go, and I discussed with her the best plan of action for Alfie's care, bearing in mind her age. She suggested that a bit of light riding until Alfie started to object would be good to keep her fit. That evening I took her out for a ride. She seemed a bit slower than usual but apart from that was fine. Imagine my surprise when the next morning she gave birth to her foal on the muck heap, surrounded by all the other very interested horses! I had been out at the time and arrived home to find Pedro standing down by the horses fence with what looked like a large dog beside him. Shocked, I suddenly realized what it was and ran down to them. Pedro had heard the horses making a lot of noise and gone to investigate. On finding Alfie giving birth in the field with all the other horses, he felt the best thing was to remove the foal, in case the other horses hurt it. I am just so glad that I hadn't gone out for the whole day, or I dread to think what would have happened if the mum and baby had been separated for more than a few minutes. Luckily everything was fine and I was able to move mum and foal into a separate paddock for a nice quiet bonding session. Little Spirit, as we named him, was tiny and obviously a bit premature, but absolutely perfect. Now, seven years later he is still very small for his age but is so sweet natured and this year we have finally started riding him, having left him a bit longer than normal to grow. He is the most adorable character, everyone's favourite, with the look of a wild horse, with his Dun colouring and markings and tatty mane which always seems to be in his eyes. He does live up to his name though, as though he is so gentle with people, and would stand and be fussed all day, when you put a saddle on him he can sometimes be a bit lively! Poor old Alfie, before we could get Leo castrated she succumbed to his charms again and the following summer produced little Fern. This time we knew exactly when the foal was due as we had written the date on the calendar, so we were quite excited at the possibility of perhaps witnessing the birth. We did get to see her come in to the world, but not quite how we had imagined! Once again Alfie decided to have her foal early.

On the day of the birth, one month before the due date, I had just picked up a head collar and was walking into the field to get Spirit with the idea of separating him from his mum in good time for the birth, as he was still having milk. Unbelievably, as I walked round the back of the stables there was Alfie, once more giving birth in the field in broad daylight (horses usually prefer to foal at night or early morning).

As you can imagine, I was quite worried as I knew the foal was early. Thankfully everything was fine and once more I was able to move Alfie and baby into the separate paddock. Unfortunately poor little Spirit didn't know what had hit him – suddenly he had a new baby sister and his mum didn't appear to love him anymore! Being small, he soon discovered that if he really persevered he could climb through the post and rail fencing to get to his mum. After placing him back in the main field several times to no avail, I decided to leave him with his mum and little sister Fern and see what happened. Alfie just ignored him, which was so confusing for poor little Spirit, but he stayed just a few feet away from them and copied everything the foal did. When Fern lay down, so did Spirit, when she ran around he ran with her, it soon became a joy to watch and it didn't take long for Alfie to accept him back, though Spirit soon found out that the milk bar was definitely out of bounds to him! Spirit and Fern soon became incredibly close, and now if Fern can't find her mum she is quite happy to go to big brother instead.

Horses are incredible to watch, especially when they live in a herd as ours do. You start to notice little things about their different characters and how they communicate with each other. They are sometimes as good as guard dogs too – you always know if someone is riding a horse by as they will all rush to the fence to have a look. Quite helpful, since until we fenced in our land completely, Scruffy liked to follow passing horses home.

One day we were able to see the amazing sight of a wild boar with her two piglets running across our land. We would have missed it if it wasn't for the horses suddenly all rushing to their fence to watch them.

We have been lucky enough to spot wild Ibex while out riding too, as the horses always see them before we do.

Our guests over the years have been fascinated by the horses and have been able to work out things about their different characters just by watching them, even if they have had no previous experience of horses.

We were quite happy with our two lovely rescue dogs, Scruffy and Suzy, and though we had sadly lost our young dog Jess, who ran off one day and never came back, we enjoyed the daily visits of Chici, her sister, our Spanish neighbours dog, who thought she lived with us too. However, a few years ago, Remes, Pedro and Gracia moved into the town, and Chici became unofficially ours, as we couldn't bear for her to be left on her own, tied up next door. It didn't make much difference to us really, as the dogs all got along very well, and Chici was always at our house anyway. In her Spanish home Chici was never allowed to go inside the house, and when she visited us she would never venture through the front door, she seemed to know that she wasn't allowed, even if she saw our dogs going in. It was so funny on the day that her old owners moved in to the village though, as she came running round to us, and straight into the kitchen – it was as if she knew that she was going to be our dog now and could go by our rules. The only problem we had was that she hadn't been spayed as our neighbours didn't agree with it at the time. Before we could do anything about it, we discovered that Chici was already pregnant, and not long after she came to live with us she gave birth to eleven puppies! She was a wonderful mum, and managed to keep them all fed, forever shifting them around to give them all a turn. Thank goodness our neighbours agreed to have her sterilised, but we were left with eleven puppies to find homes for. They were all black, but some had patches of tan or brindle. We finally found homes for all of the puppies the week before Christmas. What a horrendous depressing task that was, I felt quite desperate at times, worrying that I would never home them. They were all so cute and the older they got the more attached I got to them. With a combination of advertising and taking them to local farmers markets I gradually whittled them down, keeping one for us (how could I resist). It was sad to see them go but what an amazing episode, though never to be repeated. The site of eleven puppies running around was like something out of a Disney film. Their poor mum was incredible; to raise them all to be fat and healthy is quite an achievement. By the time they were eight weeks old she had had enough though – it was quite hysterical watching her trying to run away, with puppies clinging to her teats and dropping off all over the place as she made her get away. Scruffy and Suzy were not impressed and kept well out of the way, as did the cats, though the younger ones were happy to play sometimes.

With seven cats to choose from at the time, the puppies didn't go short of reluctant play mates. We did have only three cats until Clive found a beautiful blue eyed grey kitten in a dustbin and a few weeks later we had three more tiny kittens dumped on us. It was a very expensive time, having them all neutered, not to mention the food bill, worming, flea treatments, we actually looked into becoming a registered charity, but since that was going to cost us over one thousand euros, it was an impossible dream. As luck would have it, our guests during the puppy period were all families with small children. They thought they had gone to heaven having eleven puppies to play with and the puppies enjoyed it too. I even learned the phrase for 'can we have the puppies out' in Danish, as it was the constant cry of the three little Danish children we had staying with us. They had driven down from Denmark and were tempted to take a puppy back with them, though worried about driving all the way with such a young dog. Fate intervened half way through their holiday however, when a beautiful, pitifully thin little black dog was dumped outside the house. I could not resist feeding her as she was starving, but we decided to take her into the town and leave her where she might be more likely to find food and even a home. There was no way we could take on another dog and we were so fed up with always having to deal with stray dogs. Anyway, we took her the five kilometres into town and left her one evening and to our amazement she was back outside the following morning, having walked all the way!

Our Danish family was so impressed by what she had done, and quickly fell in love with her. She was such a gentle dog and great with the children. They desperately wanted to keep her, and used to take her out with them in the car whenever they went anywhere. I offered to ask my vet if it was possible for them to take her back to Denmark, and it turned out that all they needed was a microchip and passport, plus injections and she was free to go.

Her incredible persistence had paid off, and she went home with them to a happy life in Denmark.

-Eight-

It's me or the horses!

Unintentionally, our horse population continued to grow. We finally found a suitable horse for Elizabeth's friend Celeste, and along came Lola, a young horse, purchased locally.

She got on well with our existing horses from the start and it wasn't many months before she was officially part of our family, as for various reasons we ended up buying her.

We thought that we had now completed our horse family and certainly didn't intend to have anymore, but once more fate intervened.

One day I saw an advert for a mare and foal for sale to a good home due to their elderly owner becoming ill and unable to care for them. Once I had been to see them I couldn't leave them where they were, and soon arranged to bring Capri and Bonny home. Capri is short for Caprichosa, which means willful, and she soon lived up to her name!

Her previous owner had never ridden her and didn't know anything about her past. She seemed very placid and nice natured though, so we didn't expect any real problems. When she arrived she only had one shoe, so we rode her briefly to see how she was (and she was fine), then waited for the farrier. She proved to be incredibly scared of farriers, and had to be sedated. Farriers can be very brutal in Spain, often hitting a horse with whatever tool they have in their hand, if they don't stand still, so I was hardly surprised to learn of her fear. Following the farrier's visit we tried to ride her again, but instead of the well behaved horse she had been before, she had turned into a rearing monster! We couldn't understand it, but it seemed that she had terrible pain in her head. We called a vet, assuming she had a problem with her teeth. To our horror, the vet discovered that when the farrier had injected her, he had blown the vein in her neck, causing incredible pain in her head; it could have caused her to go blind. We changed her bridle to a bitless one to make her head more comfortable and she was soon fine. She is now a lovely horse to ride. Needless to say we never used that farrier again, and in fact it was the start of our decision to turn all the horses barefoot and bitless.

Bonny, Capri's filly, was a one year old, out of control foal when we rescued her. We were told that her Dad was a Belgium draught horse, and she certainly has that sort of stocky, strong build, she is twice the width of her mum. When she turned three, Lily started to ride her. Using Monty Roberts's methods she was able to put a saddle on her back and ride her all in one session. At the time the tack room was one of the original stables, in the horse's paddock, which meant that whenever we were moving backwards and forwards with tack, we were walking in amongst the horses. This proved to be a huge bonus with the youngsters, as being naturally inquisitive creatures, they would come up and nuzzle a saddle or bridle, as if to say "can I try it on?", and we would often pop them on them, just like small children dressing up in their mums clothes. It removed the fear without them even knowing. Within a couple of days Lily was hacking Bonny out, with me riding her mum Capri, it couldn't have been easier, all Bonny had to do was copy her mum – it was incredible. Unfortunately, the riding had to stop for a while, when we realised that she was pregnant.

Poor Bonny, her pregnancy didn't go smoothly. We didn't know when she was due, so when she started to show signs of labour we assumed that was that. Unfortunately it turned out to be pregnancy related colic. She was so ill that I spent two nights in the stable with her. The vet started talking about caesareans and told me that the foal was in the wrong position. He showed me what I would need to do if the foal started to be born the wrong way, explaining that I would have to try to push the head back in and pull the feet out!   She was in such pain that she was self harming, throwing herself against the walls over and over again. Thankfully after a couple of days it was like it had never happened and she finally had her foal a couple of weeks later, on her own, in the early hours of the morning with no problems whatsoever. The foal was so thin that we called her Twiggy – a strange name now that she has turned into a big fat thing. She is stocky and bargy just like her mum and completely adorable.

Capri was pregnant too, and gave birth to her foal Picasso a couple of weeks later. The family relationship is complicated – they all have the same dad but Capri's son is Bonny's half brother but also Twiggy's , or is he Twiggy's uncle, with Capri being Bonny's mum and Twiggy's grandmother? All very confusing.

Three foals in six weeks – how lucky! Foals thrive on having other foals to play with so it was perfect timing. The three of them and Spirit all had fun together and were very independent, though to this day they are also still very attached to their mums and on top of this, they also have their dad, Leo to play with.

Our latest addition to the adult horse population is Hercules, a wonderful English cob and a great weight carrier for heavier riders. (Also a complete teddy bear for young children to ride, unaided) He put Leo's nose out of joint when he arrived. Poor Leo was used to being the top man, and suddenly there was this big macho horse taking his girlfriends away from him. Luckily they soon got used to each other and Leo has accepted that Hercules is boss. They are now good friends and can often be seen grooming each other, though if ever Hercules is the other side of the fence, Leo still likes to try to take a sneaky bit of his bum – as long as he knows he is safe!

Having the horses is not all fun – there is constant work involved, not always pleasant.

In the winter the paddocks can become so water logged and muddy that pushing a wheelbarrow is virtually impossible. The horses love it though – you would think they were hippos the way they roll in the mud. Having clay soil, the mud then dries on their coats like cement and is virtually impossible to get off. They are happy though, which is all that matters. When we know we have riding holidays coming up, we have to make a big effort to keep them off of the mud, by putting up electric fencing, to contain them on their concrete areas, so that they still have room to move around and can walk in and out of their open stables, but at least they stay fairly mud free. If the weather gets really cold, we also put rugs on them, which is a big help in keeping them clean. We try to keep the horses as close to a natural herd as possible, and they are never confined to stables, unless it is very cold, when a couple of the older ones may get shut in at night for extra feed. They seem to thrive this way and we rarely need a vet.

Our most hated and dreaded job was getting the straw in every summer. In the early days it was only possible to buy straw for the horses to eat, no one seemed to have heard of hay, and all horses seemed to survive on it. We are lucky that Pedro grows several fields of crops and we could buy the straw from him, but this involved collecting the bales off the fields in our trailer in the July heat. You have to cover up completely, as otherwise the straw cuts you to pieces. It's horrendous; two thousand bales, with the trailer only taking twenty at a time. It's completely exhausting. Each year I expected Clive to say "it's me or the horses!" - after a full days work, the last thing he needed was to then go out collecting straw! Fortunately life has got a lot easier in recent years, and we have been able to source hay from local farmers who will deliver and stack it, which is probably just in time, as we are not getting any younger.

One year, after a terrible draught, the straw yield was much lower than usual and from early spring, until the summer harvest we had to buy in vacuum packed Golden Grass for the horses. Though expensive, it actually worked out more economical than the horrendous prices being charged for what little hay or straw was available at the time. Though very nourishing for the horses there were unexpected side effects. Because the grass has less bulk than straw, the horses eat it very quickly and are left for much of the day with nothing to eat. I tried my best to ease their boredom by cutting grass from verges and giving them tree cuttings and logs to chew as well as serving them their grass in small amounts at more frequent intervals but to our dismay they started chewing their post and rail fencing. Creosote helps to stop them chewing but unfortunately you can no longer buy it as it has been withdrawn from sale. We have electric tape around the field but they still manage to chew where they can reach without getting zapped. They chewed through both gate posts and we had to replace them with metal bar, which doesn't exactly look as good but at least is secure. This led to me having a really stupid accident; as I was getting a horse out of the gate, the metal bar touched the electric fence tape and the current went through me and then the horse, causing her to jump and stamp her foot down on the top of my foot. By that night it was very swollen, but I ignored it as I could not be bothered to go to hospital. The next day Clive and I had planned a picnic on the horses with some friends and this went ahead, with me just squeezing my foot into an old boot. As the week went on the pain increased and I had to give in and go for an x-ray. It turned out that the tendons and nerves on the top of my foot were damaged and I had to have a bandage on for ten days and rest with my foot up as much as possible; not easy with the horses to look after.

-Nine-

What have we done?

Our life here has not revolved entirely around the animals. It was our plan from the very beginning to convert two of our outbuildings into self catering accommodation to rent out for holidays. Of course, things take time and with the work involved in housing the horses and building paddocks and the pool, our renovation plans took a bit of a back seat for a while.

We finally started work on the conversions in the autumn of 2002, with the intention of being open for business by the following summer. We had a deadline of mid June, as that was when our friends' daughter Hannah, and Rebecca, (who is now John's wife), plus two friends were coming from England after finishing their exams. Four sixteen year old girls might not be everyone's idea of ideal first guests, but at least they wouldn't be too fussy if things weren't quite finished! (and our boys and their Spanish friends were more than happy about it.)

Over the years, through necessity, I had learned how to build and pride myself on being a pretty competent renderer. This was such a bonus, as Clive and I could work together at weekends, then when Clive went back to work on Monday I could be left to carry on. I have to admit that I enjoyed every minute of it and it was completely addictive. It was quite normal for us to work every night until dark, when we would make a quick meal and collapse exhausted. Sometimes my adrenalin was so high, my hands shook while I was trying to eat my dinner, I was so used to doing everything in a rush.

The buildings we were converting were very old and we were determined to keep all the rustic charm. It was a really rewarding project and we were so pleased with the end result – a quaint little two bedroom cottage.

We made it in time for the girls by the skin of our teeth, and having them as our first guests meant that we could sort out any teething problems before the 'real' guests arrived.

Advertising had been a big worry. To start with you have to make a decision on when to advertise, not knowing for sure if you are going to be ready, but needing to advertise in time to catch the summer trade. We had to stage mock up rooms, purely for the photographs, in order to get the adverts ready before the cottage was finished. Thank goodness it worked out o.k.

We were so happy that we had finally achieved our dream, but it quickly turned into a nightmare when our first official guests arrived the following week. Suddenly it was real, we had strangers staying next door and our home didn't seem our home anymore. Had we made a huge mistake?

We welcomed the lovely Irish family and showed them around, then retreated into our courtyard and hid! We were like prisoners in our own home, feeling that if we went outside we would be on display and also invade our guests' privacy. What had we done? Thankfully, we quickly got used to it, and have been very lucky to have (mostly) lovely people staying with us. It is quite normal for us to have a glass of wine with them on their patio in the evening, and a lot of guests have become good friends over the years, with many repeat bookings.

Families with children are in their element with all the animals, though one Polish family had us worried to begin with. Their two children were lovely, the eight year old girl being horse mad and loving all animals. I was slightly concerned, however, to be told that the five year old boy was terrified of animals, and that they had specifically chosen us to try to cure him of his phobia, by saturation. Thankfully it worked and by the time he went home he was happily stroking the dogs.

It has been interesting to find that though we expected to have all English guests, we actually get people from all over the world. We also get all age groups, from young couples, to families, to older couples looking for a peaceful holiday away from it all. It is certainly never boring. More recently we have tried to target people looking for riding holidays too, as a way of paying the horses keep. It is more difficult to advertise for a specific market though, but we are starting to get more riders now, though we are happy for people to come and not ride at all, if horses aren't their thing. One year we had two lovely Norwegian teenagers for a riding weekend. Their families were staying locally and as the girls were keen riders they came to stay with us in our home, to live as part of the family and ride and swim. We all had a lovely time, the boys particularly enjoying the swimming and sunbathing bit! The girls returned the following year for a whole week.

We do of course have a small income from offering riding to local people and holiday makers, and a large proportion of our cottage guests do 'have a go' at least once during their holiday, even if they are not riders. We have had some amusing episodes over the years though, with holiday makers arriving to ride, dressed in tiny shorts or on one occasion a mini skirt and flip flops!

We are very lucky to have easy, off road access to endless tracks through spectacular mountain scenery – an absolute paradise for riding. Though we do give lessons, we try whenever possible to teach as we ride in the countryside, so that everyone can benefit from the beautiful views. We cater for all levels of riders, and it is surprising how many men get roped into having a go by their 'horsey' partners. We have discovered quite a few budding riders this way; usually to their complete surprise they find that they actually enjoy it! Hercules and Lucy are a great help, they really look after their riders and seems to know just what is required.

A highlight of our guests riding holiday is often the long ride with a stop at a local restaurant for lunch in the cooler months, or an evening meal when the days are long enough in the summer. Evening rides are my favourite, as the light is so beautiful when the sun starts to fade. We usually arrive at the restaurant very hot and bursting for a nice cold beer. Clive always meets us in the Land rover with some hay for the horses and we all sit down to a very sociable meal and lots more beer of course. The ride home, often in the dark, is a memorable experience for our guests, especially if the moon is out, it is so calm and warm, with the crickets chirping, it is truly magical, and the horses really enjoy it, the cooler temperature giving them a new lease of life – galloping back down the last track is totally exhilarating.

Another enjoyable outing with the horses is the picnic ride. Again, Clive meets us with the land rover, and lots of tasty treats to eat and drink, though no need for hay this time, as the horses can happily munch the grass on the mountain side. Luckily along our riding routes we come across lots of water troughs, put there for the goats to drink from, which is very useful for us – the horses certainly appreciate them. It is a lovely, extra attraction too, when we stumble upon a herd of goats on the track and have to wade through them, feeling like cowboys. Luckily the horses are used to them, as even if they don't always see them when we are out, we can usually hear their bells tinkling on the mountain side, such a lovely, relaxing sound. Leo did get a bit upset one time though, when a goat had just given birth, and the afterbirth was still hanging – it really seemed to frighten him, poor thing, he kept turning around and trying to go home. I just get upset when I see the poor goats, so full of milk that their udders are literally dragging on the floor and swinging from side to side as they walk – it looks so painful.

One of our most spectacular picnic spots is high up on one of the mountains near the house. It can only be accessed by a steep track with a gate at the bottom and involves arranging the gate to be unlocked by the farmer. We don't do this route very often as it is too complicated, but it is worth the effort – watching the sunset over the mountains while eating a delicious picnic, drinking cava and listening to the horses happily munching on the mountain grass and herbs - absolute bliss.

-Ten-

Paxo the killer cockerel

Autumn in Spain can be a lovely time of year, but we are always aware that winter is just around the corner. The horses definitely become more of a chore, once the rain arrives – back to the mud and cancelled riding. Muddy cat and dog paw prints everywhere all add to the fun. The first rains always take us by surprise. We often get our hay covered by the skin of our teeth, when we have a freak day of rain in August.

From being on a high, having had a busy and happy summer with the horse riding, things naturally become quieter, with less holiday makers and unpredictable weather. One September, a few years ago now, we took on the task of separating the mums from their foals, to wean them. With three of them turned a year old and Leo turned four and still feeding, it was time to do something about it. We had tried to separate Picasso from Capri already, as Capri was getting too thin. We decided that we would take her to our friend's house and leave her there with their horses for a few weeks. We didn't want to do it, but felt it was best for her. Would you believe it, just hours after we left her there, she was standing outside the horse's field, having made her way home, approximately two kilometers, all on her own. After that we decided that the best option was to put all the mums in an adjoining field, so that they could still see their youngsters but couldn't feed them.

We planned to keep them apart for four weeks, but an early morning thunder storm just over three weeks into the separation had us giving in, and putting them back into the main field with the others, so that they had shelter. Thankfully the separation worked, though typically, it was Leo who made the most attempts to feed again!

I must admit to enjoying getting back into my jeans and wellies, after months of sweating in shorts and vest. I don't worry now about the horses getting cold as winter draws in, as they quickly get their warm winter coats and cope very well. I have converted their stables so that they can go in and out as they choose, with open doorways and also archways knocked through to link the stables, providing escape routes, should things get a bit rowdy. As they all live together, things are generally very relaxed. They all eat side by side and have a lovely relationship, with a definite herd hierarchy. They each seem to accept their place in the herd, though the youngsters push the boundaries (and mostly get away with it) cheekily sharing Hercules's food.

Bad weather makes looking after the horses extra hard work though - I often feel like I am living in one of those old black and white films where the family is fighting the elements, trying to get the harvest in while a monsoon is wreaking disaster – that's me on a wet and windy day, trying in vain to hold on to the tarpaulin covering the horses straw before it blows away, soaked to the skin and almost blowing away myself, or trudging through mud in my wellies, trying to feed the horses and clean them out without falling over while icy horizontal rain blasts me in the face. Life can be very hard, but there is also a satisfying feeling, when you come in from the cold and sit in front of a roaring log fire.

Talking about the problems with the tarpaulin has just reminded me of something that happened with my cockerel. The wind had torn the tarpaulin literally into shreds leaving strands of blue fibre littering the riding arena like wool. One evening when I was shutting the chickens in for the night I noticed that the poor cockerel had what looked like balls of blue wool wound round his feet. I can't imagine how he could have got into such a tangle. Anyway, I set about trying to unwind the material from his feet, thinking that he would not be too happy about it and expecting to be pecked. Unbelievably, he just sat on his perch and let me get on with it. It wasn't a quick task, but he seemed to know that I was helping him. The chickens are funny creatures, and usually quite scared, running off squawking at the slightest thing. Choco (a water dog that we gave a home to, though sadly only briefly) used to send them into a frenzy if he even as much as walked near them. Poor Choco, he was such a gentle giant and he didn't want to hurt them but they didn't understand that. Mind you, Choco was in the dog house for a different reason – I thought that some of the hens had stopped laying as we were getting very few eggs, that was until I found him in the hen house, eating the eggs – I wonder how many more he had eaten? The hole into the chicken shed is quite small, and I had no idea that Choco could fit through it. I'm sure that too many eggs can't be good for a dog, so I had to be careful after that. It was bad enough that I had an egg mad horse to contend with. Lola always follows me round to the chicken shed and hangs about outside hopefully – she loves eggs and will eat one whole, shell and all, taking it straight from my hand. Apparently it doesn't do a horse any harm to have the odd egg so I do occasionally give in to her – its fun to watch her bite in to it and dribble it every where. The other horses always think they are missing out on a treat and have all tried an egg, but none of the others like them. Keeping chickens can be quite worrying, we have had them all murdered by foxes twice now, it is quite devastating when it happens, and all because we forget to shut them in at night, we feel so terrible. Over the years we have had a few cockerels, usually the typical children's picture book type, with the black feathers with touches of rust and green, always handsome creatures with large spurs, strutting around like they own the place and keeping the hens in tow, and quite meek and gentle in their behavior towards us. Once, though, when we had to replace all of the chickens after a visit from a fox, I made the mistake of taking pity on a very sad looking cockerel, squashed into a small cage, and though not the usual type we went for, decided to take him. He was very striking, being speckled black and white and he seemed fine for a few weeks, quickly adapting to his new home and taking charge of his harem of hens. Unfortunately his behavior soon started to change, and he became a monster. No one was safe from him; guests lived in fear of his attacks and often went into the garden armed with a stick or a rake or something they could use to fend him off. He could be innocently pecking the garden when you went past, but would suddenly turn and run after you, jumping up and attacking with his spurs, he was truly frightening. Even now, the sound of scuttling feet on gravel still makes my heart start beating faster. We had a lovely Slovakian girl staying with us at the time, helping with the garden. Poor Jana, being bent over, weeding, she was a constant target, she hated him. She would say, in her lovely, musical accent - "The cock, he no like me, and I'm a vegetarian", it did make us laugh. When she left she made us promise that if we ever killed him, we would invite her back so that she could eat him, despite not being a meat eater, she hated him that much. We named him Paxo, as though we didn't want to admit it we knew that he was destined for the dinner table. I tried every thing to tame him, looking up solutions on the internet. I would try cuddling him in the hen house before letting him out in the morning, which he accepted without a struggle, but made no difference whatsoever. I then tried to mimic his behavior, another of the suggestions, by chasing him, showing my dominance, again, no change. I then tried doing the cockerel dance, how stupid I must have looked to anyone watching, walking sideways, turning my head away, stopping when he stopped, it was all great fun, but none of it worked. I persevered for months, not wanting to admit defeat, but after he had attacked a three year old guest he had to go. I asked Remes to come and get him, knowing that it would not be a problem for her to do the dreaded deed. He let me pick him up and hand him over to Remes, it was very sad, but I had tried my best. Poor Paxo.

Our neighbours have been involved in our lives quite a lot over the years; we certainly couldn't have managed without them, especially in the early days. Gracia is the first person the kids turn to if they have a problem, she is like an older sister. When Lily was younger she would often go round to their house for lunch if they were cooking a vegetarian meal and we even had to give in and allow Remes and Gracia to take her to get her ears pierced on her tenth birthday, despite not planning to allow it until she was at least sixteen! In Spain it is usual for babies to have their ears pierced, so we felt that now that Lily was living in here, we couldn't really say no. The year I celebrated my fortieth birthday, Gracia was insistent that I should go out 'on the town' in Trabuco with her and her friends, to celebrate. It was a great night, starting at 10pm with a meal, followed by a disco pub but I had to admit defeat at two thirty am. My dad had also arranged to take me skiing for my birthday, just the two of us, much to the disgust of the kids who were desperate to come too. Dad was insistent that it was to be my treat and in any case they all had school that day. The kids all set off on the school bus that morning, while I waited for Dad to arrive, but before we could set off for the ski slopes we had a phone call to say that the school had been closed and they had to come home. I was quite familiar with this, as it was quite common for children to put silicone in the school locks so that school would be canceled for the day, but I though that it was taking it a bit far to arrange for this to happen just so that they could come skiing with me! The kids soon arrived home in a frenzy of excitement – it turned out that Harry had been the first person to walk into the school, and had found a dead body hanging out of a sky light window. He was so hyped up about it, saying that he hadn't been scared at all and wanted to work in police forensics when he left school. The poor dead man had been trying to rob the school canteen and had become stuck in the window and suffocated.

It often comes as a big surprise to Expats that the winters here in the mountainous inland regions of southern Spain can be a bit colder than they imagined. With our house being at eight hundred metres above sea level it can be a lot colder than it is on the coast. Over the years we have learnt how to manage, and can now keep the house quite cosy, with a wood burner one end and a roaring open fire in the other. We don't bother to heat our own bedrooms, as long as the bed is warm it doesn't matter as far as we're concerned – and our bedroom has dropped as low as eight degrees centigrade! It is always hard work though, for us to ensure that our guests are warm when it gets really cold. We do spoil them by providing thick quilts and extra throws and cosy wood burners, but it can come as a bit of a shock to holiday makers expecting hot sunny Spain all year round. Having said that, we are incredibly lucky when the sun does shine, with lovely hot sunny days in the depth of winter. We decided a few years ago that we were frustrated with our guests being able to sunbathe in lovely hot temperatures from September to June, but not being able to use the pool. We made the decision to buy a pool heater and it has been a real bonus. We do struggle a little bit to keep the pool at twenty eight degrees when it is really cold, but most of the time it works really well. We couldn't have chosen a worse winter to have it installed though – December to February 2004/5 must have been the coldest on record. When we started heating the pool that December, little did we know what was in store; trying to heat a pool in temperatures of minus ten is not easy.

It was hard enough for the house to cope – thank goodness that we didn't have guests staying the day the pipes froze. Sadly lots of people lost precious plants that had been growing for decades, it was such a shame.

It was a nightmare for the horses as well, with their water trough being frozen every day.

How amazing the snow was though. We couldn't believe it when it started snowing and actually settled quite deep on the ground. The horses were fascinated – it must have been the first snow they have ever seen. It was lovely to see them with snow on their backs – a sure sign that they were warm and not losing any body heat through their coats. It was such fun watching the Spanish out enjoying it too, we hadn't had snow in Trabuco for fifty years, so most of them had never seen it before, and were really making the most of it, building snow men and throwing snow balls.

Despite the occasional extreme weather, a good side effect of living in Spain, I have found, is that you don't seem to suffer from the January blues that is so often a problem in England. At least we have plenty of sunny days here and that feeling that spring is just around the corner.

I do enjoy the novelty of the cold weather when it first arrives though, it's lovely and cosy when you have that first log fire, but with the extra cold winters of the last couple of years, firewood (or lack of it) soon becomes a worry. It's incredible how much you get through. We have thought about central heating in the past, but our house is very old with thick stone walls and keeps quite warm. It would be a shame to spoil the old walls by installing pipes and radiators, so we cope with open fires and gas heaters and the odd electric panel heater. Of course you do need enough electricity – something a lot of expats struggle with. We only survive now as we have had our own transformer installed to upgrade our supply. Winter is much more expensive than the summer for running the guest cottages. Of course there is a lot more electricity used, with the heaters in the cottages and the pool heater, but we also provide free wood for the log burners. Firewood is very expensive and it is so frustrating to witness some guests sitting out on their patios with the door open and the wood burner lit – one guest actually told us that though they didn't really need the heat, they liked the country cottage atmosphere the fire gave! Running guest accommodation is very rewarding but it can also be frustrating and upsetting at times, and you do have to be very tolerant of people's idiosyncrasies.

-Eleven-

Goodbye Rocky

Our summers are always hectic and tiring, with lots of friends from England visiting, and often providing meals for guests, it's one long social whirl. It's always great fun and we wouldn't have it any other way, but keeping up with the late nights (shooting star watching competitions by the pool) and still getting up early to see to the horses takes its toll. Autumn and winter bring a bit of a rest in comparison, though I do admit that I often feel a bit lonely. It was worse when the kids were all at home, and went back to college. With Clive out working I was suddenly back to being on my own. I usually solved my boredom by starting a new decorating project. A few years ago, when John left for England for his brief spell in the army, he suggested that I could knock down his bedroom wall and extend the kitchen. Of course I said don't be silly, and assured him that his room would always be there waiting for him. The trouble was, the seed was sown, and I soon started to like his idea. Within weeks of him leaving I had knocked down his bedroom wall and had a lovely new L–shaped kitchen. Little did I know then, that fourteen months later he would be back, with no bedroom to come home to. We solved the problem by converting the kid's den above Clive's shed to a little studio apartment for him, so he did alright out of his clever idea in the end.

The DIY over the years has been continuous. Though our house was perfectly habitable from the start, it lacked character and modern conveniences. We were lucky when we moved in that my parents were having a new fitted kitchen installed. We had their old units and once painted with new marble worktops, and a large shiny pine table sanded down to bare wood, the kitchen had just the right farm house feel. We have always enjoyed decorating and furnishing our homes from old furniture either donated from family or found in junk shops, car boot sales or auctions. I get more pleasure from renovating old furniture than I ever would from buying new. I have also always loved sewing, which saves us a lot of money – I like to buy whole bolts of fabric and make cushions, curtains, pool sun beds, even covering sofas, I have often joked that I would make us all clothes to match, like the Von Trap family in the Sound of Music! Inside the house there wasn't much more to do, just building wardrobes and extra bathrooms and generally giving it a homely rustic feel that it lacked. Outside was a different story, over the years as well as converting the barns into the guest cottages and building the stables and pool, we have gradually knocked down outbuildings to extend our courtyard and landscaped the gardens – just a pea field when we moved in. It has been constant hard work, but very rewarding. We like to think that one day we will finish and sit back to enjoy the results but I doubt it. At least we have been able to do all the work ourselves, which has saved us an incredible amount of money, and we have also had some lucky finds, such as beautiful old wooden doors on rubbish tips etc.

In hindsight we have realised that it is a good idea not to rush straight into things. Ideas we had when we first arrived were put on hold for one reason or another, but actually turned out to be for the best, as new ideas were much better.

The garden is now taking shape, but with the water shortages of the past few years we have had to concentrate on just providing enough water to keep the plants alive, meaning that they haven't flourished as much as they could have done. One thing that grows in the winter time is grass. To start with this was a problem as we did not intend to have any and saw it as a nuisance, forever trying to weed it out from between the plants. I finally realised that it would be best to stop fighting it and started to keep it strimmed down. It now provides us with a lovely green lawn effect between the shrubs, the mix of grass and weeds all looking the same when cut short. By June it is yellow until the first rains of the autumn but it still looks neat and tidy. Its a nightmare in early spring though, when I do the first cut as I am literally down on my hands and knees sifting through the grass looking for bulb shoots, so as not to strim them down. Of course I never find them all and sadly cut a few bulbs which is such a shame. This year I have taken photos of all the bulbs to use as a guide next year.

We had a very strange and annoying incident one spring; I have planted bulbs in the verge outside our house, daffodils being one thing I miss from England, I was keen to see them flowering in my garden. Unfortunately someone else thought they looked pretty too and actually dug up a whole clump, still in flower. I was so upset; I wish I could have seen who did it.

Another problem we have to contend with in the garden is the chickens. I love the way they wander around, pecking the ground, they look so funny, but they can be so destructive. When I bought my first lot of hens I was asked if I wanted their beaks cut, something that horrified me and I said no. These hens were a menace and cut off all my flower heads using their beaks like scissors. When I had to replace them I could only buy hens with cut beaks which at the time saddened me but I feel very guilty to admit that they are so much better for the garden! Now my flowers stay in one piece, but the hens still love to dig the soil and often dig up anything newly planted. Clive's biggest bug bear is the horses eating the garden. We have grown a mixed hedge around their field and sometimes when the wind blows they are able to reach the trees and bite the tops off. They are also fond of taking a bite of any tree they pass when we set off to ride, Hercules being the keenest tree eater. Clive despairs of ever having a decent garden —he really has the patience of a saint, especially as he is not quite the animal lover that I am.

A few years ago we were lucky enough to have an advert for the Audi A4 filmed at our house. It was in May and the weather on the run up to the weekend chosen for filming was perfect. The film company was busy building a mock up of an antiques shop on the end of the house; you wouldn't believe the amount of work that goes in to filming an advert that lasts just a few seconds. Typically, on the day of filming the weather changed and we had torrential rain with mud every where. The catering lorry that was parked on our threshing circle got bogged down in the mud and had to be towed out, leaving muddy ruts for us to sort out. Just to add insult to injury, we never did see the advert, though it was apparently shown on one of the Spanish satellite stations.

The weather is never predictable, some years we have terrible drought, year after year, but then again, we can also have several winters in a row where it feels like it does nothing but rain. We always have to conserve water though, not least because it is very expensive, and this summer we struck lucky. Jose Manuel was doing some work on his olives, in his field that borders our land. He had a digger putting drainage in, and discovered a very wet patch of ground, right near our fence. He suggested it would be a good idea to investigate further, as he was sure that when he lived in our house as a child, the field was always wet in this particular area. We borrowed his digger and sure enough, we found water underground. What a bit of luck, we were able to put in some grey concrete tubes and create our own well, to use for the horses drinking water. To be on the safe side we had the water analised and it is perfectly safe for the horses to drink. Hopefully our water bills will be a bit cheaper from now on.

In Spain you often come across water 'depositos' in the countryside; man-made water storage to help with watering plants etc. Unfortunately these can be deadly to any animals unlucky enough to fall in. A few years ago we received the saddest news from my parents – their beautiful, loveable Spanish water dog Rocky had drowned in a neighbor's deposito. He loved water so much, and on the day he died he was out for a walk with my Dad and just disappeared. Dad called him but to no avail, and eventually gave up and went home, thinking that Rocky would be there waiting for him as if to say 'where have you been', as he often used to do. Sadly he never made it home, he must have decided it would be fun to have a swim, but the deposito had steep slippery sides, and once he was in, it was impossible for him to get out again. Even now it is so hard to come to terms with; he really was the most unique dog. The gap he has left is impossible to fill, but he will never be forgotten. My parents acquired him by accident really, when they first moved to Spain. As a pup he belonged to the local goat herd who passed their house in Sedella daily. Rocky always ran up to the house to say hello and Mum and Dad soon came to love him. One day the goat herd asked them if they would like him, as he was such a stupid lovable clown, he really wasn't much good at herding goats. Of course they jumped at the chance and Rocky soon became a much loved part of our family. He was so funny when the goat herd came past after that, he would hide as if to say 'I'm not going back there.' He loved to come over and visit us to play with all our animals, barking at the horses, chasing the chickens, he was in his element. He would never hurt a thing though, he was so gentle. When my parents rescued a kitten Rocky would carry it around in his mouth like it was his baby. Scruffy, our male dog hated him of course, and watched him like a hawk, waiting for him to do something wrong so that he could join in with the 'Oh Rocky!' by barking at him, telling him off along with us. Mum and Dad always said that after a visit to us Rocky would sulk for a day, obviously missing the mayhem, but he loved Mum and Dad to bits, and was very happy being an 'only dog'. He was very spoiled but never badly behaved – everyone loved him, he really was the kindest, silliest most loving dog that anyone had ever met. When you went to visit, Rocky was there at the car door ready to welcome you with his madly wagging stump of a tail. Mum and Dad can only comfort themselves with the fact that Rocky had six really happy years, with a warm loving home that he wouldn't have had if he had remained a goat dog. His funny, friendly face always comes to mind when you think of him, he will never be forgotten.

Since Rocky's death, Mum and Dad have acquired two more water dogs called Luca and Mitch, they will never replace Rocky and have totally different characters, but they each have their own charm and help to fill the void that Rocky left.

It is certainly not difficult to acquire a new dog in Spain, there are so many strays and the rescue centres are full to bursting, it is so sad. The recession has made their plight worse, with lots of Expats having to sell up and move back to their countries, leaving their animals behind. The Spanish are also renowned for just dumping their dogs in the streets when they go on holiday, or if the hunting season has finished. It is a problem that is never going to go away, and though most of the stray dogs are timid and make lovely, grateful, loyal pets if given a chance, of course a lot are starving, and this can lead to other problems.

We had experience of the damage stray dogs can do to another animal when our goats were attacked. It was in the summer and luckily the bedroom window was open. I was suddenly woken up by the sound of frenzied dog barking. Our dogs in the house had heard it too, and were barking to go out and investigate. I ran outside and could hear that the barking was coming from the direction of the goats. Then I heard the most terrible crying sound, it still haunts me now. I just ran blindly in the dark with bare feet, ignoring the cactus thorns and stones, my heart pounding. As I approached the goat pen it was obvious by the noise that the goats were being attacked by stray dogs. I just screamed and shouted as loud as I could as I entered the pen, and thank goodness the dogs ran off, squeezing under the wire fence. In the dark I couldn't see if the goats were hurt, but I ran my hands over them and they seemed o.k. Fudge felt wet around her neck but I put that down to saliva. I pushed them into their shed and shut them in, just in case the dogs came back, and went back to bed. To my horror, when I turned on the light to wash my hands I discovered that they were covered in blood. Armed with Clive and a torch this time, I ran back down to the goats to see what was wrong. Poor Fudge, her injuries were terrible, it looked like the dogs had been trying to tear her throat out. Holly had been luckier, with only a small cut on her back. I cleaned them up as best I could and rang the vet. Thankfully, after a week of having to give them daily injections they were both fine, but what a frightening experience.

For the next few weeks we had to shut the goats in every night, which they weren't too happy about. We did locate the owner of the dogs, who promised to keep them under control in future, but it has left me very worried, every time I hear a dog bark at night.

As if we haven't got enough problems, Clive has got it into his head to rear a couple of pigs for meat. Considering that apart from a couple of the cats, I'm sure Clive could quite cheerfully say goodbye to all our animals, we really should humour him in this latest challenge. There is a small problem though (and no, it's not the smell, as apparently if you keep them clean they are not too bad). No, it's the fact that Elizabeth is a vegetarian and I also know for a fact that I will not cope easily with killing Pinky and Perky! With the best intensions in the world, the pigs will become pets, and though I am trying to convince myself that the pigs would have a good life with us, and would be destined for meat any way, I know I would find it impossible to allow them to be killed. After the years of dry hot summers and wet winters, making life so much harder with the animals, we seem to have turned the corner. They all look lovely and healthy and happy and have settled in to a nice routine and are quite often the highlight of the holiday for our guests, who often make comments in the guest book to that effect. It is so lovely to see little children who live in London with no pets delight in having a dog outside their door when they wake up in the morning, or a cat sleeping on the cane over their patio. Of course they love to help groom the horses or feed the goats, and collecting the eggs is a firm favourite, though I have lost count of how many eggs have been dropped by little hands on the way up from the field to show Mum and Dad.

Guests often comment that we should make more of the fact that we have the animals on our website, but we have to explain that as not all people feel the same about animals it is difficult as we aim to please everyone, and if guests don't like dogs then we are more than happy to keep them in our own courtyard so that they don't bother them. (And we certainly don't allow them to bark all day as we know how annoying that can be.) In the recession we value every single holiday booking and tailor each holiday to suit the guest, so that if they are not animal people then they won't have to worry about them and visa versa. We are very aware that animals can put some people off, we were actually asked recently by some Norwegians who were making a holiday enquiry if we allowed our dogs to swim in the pool! A chance would be a fine thing as they are all scared of it, and anyway the pool is gated, but sadly they decided not to book, despite our assurances, as they had not enjoyed a previous experience in a villa where the owner's dogs were given free run of the pool. Oh well, you can't win them all, but we do try our hardest to.

-Twelve-

A mouse party

When we first started letting our rental cottages our main business tended to be in the summer months, but in recent years we have been lucky enough to be booked up all year round. It is great to have guests here to enjoy the different seasons, as though the summer is beautiful, with the predictable weather, it is hard to beat the spring in Andalucia,
I think it is my favourite time of year. Our garden is in its prime, with the daffodils and tulips and the fruit tree blossom, it is so colourful, you always forget how beautiful it is, after a long hot summer and muddy winter, and it comes as a lovely surprise every year. Of course it is hard work, there is always more to do in the garden in the spring, but it is the best time of year to be outside. I always think it's a shame that most people only see Spain in the summer and never get to experience the wonders of spring here. The horses all start to shed their thick winter coats too, transforming them from muddy woolly monsters back to the beautiful creatures that have been hiding all winter.
The birds love all the molting hair, using it to build their nests. The stables are full of sparrow and swallows nests. I love watching the birds busily preparing their homes, but sadly I often discover tiny just hatched baby birds on the stable floors.

Taking a walk in the countryside at this time of year is breathtaking. The wild flowers are so incredible. On the mountainside where we live you can see wild peonies, orchids, iris and the fields are full of wild gladioli and poppies. Some years there are so many poppies that the fields appear red. Add to this glorious picture the bright yellow of the broom and gorse against the green of the crops in the fields and the effect is stunning.

A draw back of spring is the Processionary caterpillars. You will see their nests in pine trees from about December; they look like thick white spiders webs. They hatch in the spring and they can be deadly to animals. You can recognise them easily as they move around in processions (hence the name) nose to tail in a long train. They can be removed from the trees by sealing a plastic bag around the nest and cutting off the branch but you have to be really careful. If a dog or cat sniffs the caterpillar or plays with it, the injuries can be horrific, with animals losing their tongues if they are really unlucky.

Our guests at this time of year are often walkers and nature lovers and are in their element here. One year, one of our guests decided to go for a long walk up to the top of the mountain behind our house. He set off on his own, taking a picnic and a few instructions from us for finding his way to the top. Unbeknown to us, our dog Scruffy had sneaked off with him. I didn't realise this until I noticed that Scruffy had been missing for a few hours, and then I guessed what had happened. When the guest came back I went out to apologise to him for Scruffy tagging along. It turned out that Scruffy had actually saved the day. The walk had started off well, with Scruffy happily walking along with our guest, who was actually quite pleased to have some company. After they had been walking for a couple of hours and were half way up the mountain they came to a fenced off area with a gate. Our guest decided to leave Scruffy the other side of the gate and pick him up on the way back, rather than try to lift him over, as the mountain was starting to get steeper. As he climbed over Scruffy had other ideas, and found a gap in the fence to squeeze through. This turned out to be a blessing, as a little bit further up were some very fierce dogs. Apparently our guest was just thinking that he would have to turn back, when good old Scruffy started barking at them and keeping them out of the way, so that our guest could carry on walking. When they got to the top of the mountain he shared his lunch with Scruffy and they made their way home. As our guest recounted his story, it was obvious that he had thoroughly enjoyed their little adventure, and that Scruffy had enhanced the experience. Perhaps we should start renting him out as a guide!

Here in Spain we like to celebrate the Saints days, with each town choosing a few Saints each year to celebrate as their own, on top of the national holidays. April the twenty fifth, dia de St. Marcos, is celebrated in Villanueva del Trabuco and the surrounding area each year in a big way. On the weekend nearest to the day itself, the campo starts to fill up with tents until it seems like the whole village is camping or picnicking in the country side. It's an amazing sight and causes great excitement during the preparations, especially amongst the young adult population who seize the chance to be independent from their parents and camp with their friends. Our children were no exception and the planning started well before the event, with decisions to be made about who they would be camping with, and where to pitch their tents. Then of course there was the food shopping and raiding of the kitchen for anything to boost their hoard. Some years they were lucky and the weather was glorious, with the kids and their friends sneaking home for a quick swim in the pool. At other times the torrential rain stopped play, resulting in early morning Land Rover rescues of soggy teenagers, and the towing out of cars bogged down in the mud. Not deterred, and ever optimistic, the plans are made each year and fingers are firmly crossed. With perhaps the exception of the main annual fiesta, the St Marcos celebrations are the highlight of the year. We have been lucky enough to share in Pedro, Remes and Gracia's family picnic most years, which is a very enjoyable way of experiencing true Spanish life, with mountains of lovely home made food (Remes makes a wonderful Spanish omelette) and the chance to sample the home made chorizo from the winter Matanzas (or pig killings) which occur frequently in the surrounding farms during the colder weather. The day of the killing is like a party, with the whole extended family arriving to help prepare the various delicacies provided by the pig. I have to admit to not accepting an invitation myself – just the sound of the poor pig squealing in the distance is enough to put me off, though I know that the squeal is just from the panic of the chase, and that the killing is quite humane.

A focal point of the camping and picnicking is Los Cien caños, the water source at the foot of the mountain behind our house, five kilometres outside of Villanueva del Trabuco, just off of the Zafarraya/Los Alazores road. This is a very popular tourist attraction at any time of year, with day trippers from the towns and coast driving out to see the source of the Guadalhorce river that flows into Malaga. The hundred pipes sticking out of the mountain side are quite an incredible sight, with the water gushing out like a waterfall in the winter. Recently our local Mayor has caused a bit of a stir in the village, in relation to that particular part of the mountain side. Being National Park area, it has recently undergone a bit of an overhaul, to promote rural tourism, with new sign posts and marked walkways, and the Cien Caños has been declared an area of Natural Beauty. Bearing this in mind, you can imagine the uproar when the Mayor decided to purchase land belonging to a family member, right in front of the water pipes, and employ yet more family members, to build a huge, ugly picnic area, with about sixty wooden picnic benches all in regimental rows. It is an unbelievable white elephant. No one can imagine who is going to want to picnic there, and though there are new trees planted for shade, it is going to be at least ten years before they are big enough to be of any use, that's if it survives that long, as there is every chance that all the fresh loose soil will be washed down the mountain side with the first winter rains.

A slight down side to the St Marcos fiesta is that we get a lot of people streaming past our farm on their way to the site. This in itself is not a problem, but for that particular weekend we do start to feel a bit like public property, with cars slowing down to stare at the horses and sometimes actually pulling in to park on our cobbled threshing circle, to wander down with their children to see the horses. Though we do take people horse riding by appointment, our land is private property and is quite obviously a landscaped garden, with many plants, trees and flowers. It is slightly frustrating to have people wandering around as if it is common land. Oh well, its only once a year and it is natural for people to want to show their children the horses, we just wish that they would ask first. We have recently fenced all of our land off, which should solve the problem. It is not that we are anti- social, but we have our guests to think of, and also we do not want the responsibility of other people's children let loose with the horses. If there was an accident, we would get the blame. Actually, to be fair, sometimes when we have had big parties for our children's birthdays when they were younger, there were so many cars on the threshing circle that passers by stopped to enquire if we were a restaurant. One year for Elizabeth's birthday we staged a Cintas competition with the horses for the kids, and even put up fiesta bunting. Quite understandably on this occasion it did cause a bit of confusion among passers by, some of whom stopped and wandered down to the field, thinking it was a genuine fiesta. My dad has often said that we should put some tables out and serve cream teas! Recently I did have cause to take exception to one particular large, expensive looking passing car. Its middle aged Spanish occupants actually stopped and started to pick my flowers from the verge by the road. I have had daffodils stolen in the past, much to my distress, but this time I was actually witnessing the couple quite blatantly helping themselves to my marigolds. When I approached them and explained that they were picking flowers that I had planted myself on my land, they actually had the nerve to stand and argue with me, saying that the land was by the road and they were within their rights to pick the flowers. I pointed out that the plants and flowers there were quite obviously not wild and were bought at garden centres, some even still had tags on. I explained that it was pointless picking them anyway as they would be dead tomorrow. They merely argued that they wanted to dry them, and carried on picking them. I couldn't believe what I was seeing. They said that they were from Malaga, though why they thought that would excuse their behavior I have no idea – it was as if the fact that they came from a built up city gave them the right to help themselves to flowers from the countryside. I really don't want to start putting signs up but it is very upsetting when people don't respect your privacy. Oh well, I suppose it is a very English thing to be possessive of your property; I will just have to try to relax a bit.

Spring time brings another type of problem for us – mice! One spring after a heavy spell of rain the mice decided that they would move into our bedroom. We have never had problems before or since (and luckily no problems at all in the guest accommodation), but our bedroom is upstairs in the part of the house that was used in the past for grain storage. With the ceiling and floor being constructed of beams and cane, it is easy for small holes to appear, and mice can get through spaces so tiny you wouldn't think it possible. To start with I would hear the odd scratching, but when I whispered to Clive, or turned on a torch, it always stopped. After a while though, the mice stopped trying to hide their presence, and on one occasion I turned on my lamp to see a very cute one sitting on my bedside table. They stopped being quiet and started to party, squeaking as if they were laughing at us. We tried poison, but that was a big mistake as they would then die under the bed and we would only find them when they started to rot. We bought an expensive electronic mouse repeller, but that was useless. Finally we resorted to old fashioned traps, which did the trick. We didn't sleep for weeks, it really was a nightmare. We have now sealed up every little hole we can find, and so far it hasn't been a problem.

-Thirteen-

What a shock!

One spring we had to deal with a much more traumatic incident. There are electricity cables suspended high across our land, supplying the farms on the mountain opposite us. One day Clive noticed that one of the cables looked very frayed. We showed our neighbor, but he said that it wasn't a problem as there was a strong inner core, and that it wouldn't break, so we thought no more of it. A couple of months later after a horrendous night of thunderstorms, resulting in a power cut, I went down in the morning to feed the horses and my blood ran cold – laying on the ground in the middle of the horses field was a live electric cable. The power was still off, but we had no way of knowing if the service engineers might try to re- connect at any time, not knowing what had occurred. I watched with my heart in my mouth as Clive used his electrician's pliers to get hold of the large cable and drag it out of the field. One of the young horses, Twiggy, had panicked and had her legs caught up in it and my stomach was doing somersaults, waiting for Clive to remove the cable to safety. It really was one of the most frightening moments of my life. We rang the electricity company and four hours later they eventually turned up, and had the cheek to tell Clive off for touching the cable – apparently it was a very dangerous thing to do – Ha! Ha! Clive would not have dreamt of it if he hadn't had the correct tools, but it makes you wonder what would have happened if we had just sat back and waited for the authorities to get round to doing something. I recently had a run in with electricity myself, on a much smaller scale. My parents were celebrating their golden wedding and we were holding a surprise party for them at our house. The preparations were huge, with Lily flying home from Germany and lots more relatives arriving from the Uk, it was very difficult to keep it secret. We also had lots of their local friends coming for the actual party on the Saturday night. Being early March, the weather leading up to the weekend was glorious, as we rushed around, getting the house ready for all the guests, preparing food and decorations. Our first guests were due to arrive on the Thursday evening and the actual day was lovely and warm and sunny, we were able to put all the cushions out on the outside sofas and make the farm look as inviting as possible. We couldn't believe our luck, but were very relieved, after all the hard work we had put in. We enjoyed a lovely meal with my brother, sister and family and at seven a.m on the Friday morning Clive packed them all into the Landover and set off to The Sierra Nevadas for a day skiing. I stayed behind to collect more guests from the airport and was just seeing Clive off when it started to thunder and the heavens opened. In a panic, though it was still dark, I ran down to the horses field, to get them all off of the mud and onto the concrete areas, as I was expecting riding guests at the end of the weekend and couldn't let the horses get wet and muddy. It was a total nightmare, being on my own, I didn't know which way to turn, running around the field with lightening crashing all around me, trying to move all the electric fence posts and tape to contain the horses on the concrete. I had turned off the switch on the battery before I started and was just in the process of re-threading the electric tape on to the posts in their new position when I got the most almighty electric shock; with the ground being wet it was much stronger than normal. I screamed out and looked over to the battery, not understanding how it had happened, when I had definitely turned it off, only to see Buffy the cat, rubbing herself against the switch – she had obviously turned it back on! Just to add to my problems, it then started snowing and was soon a blizzard, I could hardly see my hand in front of my face. I couldn't believe what was happening! I finally got the horses sorted out, and just had enough time to prepare lunch ready for later and get myself cleaned up before setting off for the airport at ten a.m. By the time I got to the motorway the road was almost in- passable, the snow had fallen so quickly, it was unbelievable, and very frightening. My hands were shaking as I gripped the steering wheel and desperately tried to see where I was going. Luckily, as I drove down towards Malaga the snow turned to heavy rain, but it was really miserable. When I got back home with my cousins they couldn't believe their eyes, they had to trudge through inches of wet melting snow to get from the house to the car – I was very glad that I had made soup for lunch. Oh well, it all added to the excitement and we had a lovely cosy evening by the fire when everyone got back from skiing. Unbelievably the next day dawned bright and sunny and we were able to have a paella lunch outside in the courtyard before preparing for the party in the evening. It was a lovely weekend and my parents were genuinely surprised. Part of our preparations for the weekend had involved renovating what was Johns apartment above Clive's workshop into a proper guest apartment to use for our full board horse riding clients and shorter breaks. As we had so many family members staying we needed the extra space and it was good to have a deadline to complete the work, though it wasn't so much fun working until eleven p.m every night in the last week , to be ready in time. We were so thrilled with the finished result though, and thanks to Ikea, which had recently opened in Malaga, we were able to furnish it simply and stylishly, in keeping with the rustic effect of the old building. During the recession when things were at their worst, we had had to resort to having people to stay in our own farmhouse, often completely shutting off one end of the house so that we were confined to our kitchen/living area with one bedroom and use of the courtyard shower, so that we could make a bit more rental income from letting the rest of the house. We hated it though, knowing that people were in our home, using our things, (and not always sympathetically) it was something we had to do, but we knew that we would have to come up with an alternative for the future, to get our lives back.

Our new El Jaral apartment has proved to be a very popular replacement to the farmhouse b and b, and though it shares our courtyard, it has its own entrance and guests have a lot more privacy. They also have a kitchen to prepare meals, which means they can either stay with us on a self catering basis, or they can have evening meals in the Farmhouse dining room or outside in the summer. Only a couple of years previously we had built our second guest cottage, El Establo. Clive's building work had started to dry up and we were struggling to make ends meet. The obvious solution seemed to be to convert another guest cottage, as each week we could let out would be the equivalent of a week's wages for Clive. This cottage was built where we originally had an old barn that was Polly's first stable when she first arrived. Unfortunately the barn was not good enough to renovate and had to be knocked down, but the plan was to rebuild, making it look like an old building that had always been there. It certainly wasn't easy to build, being off of our outer courtyard area, only accessed by a small gateway. It was impossible to get any machinery in, other than a mini digger to dig the footings. All the concrete and materials had to be wheel- barrowed in, from the threshing circle, through the courtyard, all the while having to be quiet and tidy so as not to disturb any guests staying in the original cottage. We were constantly having to wait for guests to go out so that we could use a power tool, it was certainly a juggling act, and we all became incredibly fit, with the countless wheel barrow loads of concrete we pushed, and uphill, just to add to the burden. How we managed to mix up and lay the complete footings in one day still amazes me, but I suppose it had to be done and we had no choice. Once more, we had a deadline as it was the year that our eldest son John was getting married and we needed the extra accommodation for the wedding guests. It was all hands on deck; as usual we worked every day until late into the evening, desperately trying to get finished in time for the August deadline. On top of this we had the wedding to prepare for, not to mention looking after the horses and taking guests riding, plus preparing meals for guests from time to time, as well as the general maintenance, changeovers, pool cleaning, painting and gardening. Though the actual ceremony was to be held at a local hotel, we were hosting a large evening reception here at the farm, so not only did we need the cottage finished, but we needed the whole outer area to look good for the wedding - the pressure was really on! We did manage to get the cottage habitable enough for all the teenagers to camp out in, with a usable shower room, thanks to our friends grouting the tiles two days before! One of my main memories is of desperately scrubbing my builder's hands in an effort to make them presentable on the morning of the wedding, how I wished that evening gloves were still in fashion. Oh well, who would be looking at my hands anyway?

Imagine how we felt just a few days after the wedding, when all the horses broke out of their field and were happily munching the garden as we came out in the morning to feed them, we could only be thankful that it didn't happen just a few days earlier. Once the wedding was over and we had enjoyed a nice rest with our friends it was back to the grindstone. As with our first cottage, we had to decide on a date to have the cottage ready by, in order to begin advertising, so we settled on the October half term. To add to the pressure, Clive had a bit of much needed building work to do for friends which left me home alone, trying to carry on with the cottage as best I could. The strain of the twelve hour days was starting to take its toll – we were both physically and mentally exhausted, not only from the heavy work load, but the financial worry of the project too, especially being so soon after the wedding. On top of that we were barely eating as we were so tired by the time we finished each night at about ten o'clock, that we often just had some egg on toast or something quick before stumbling in to bed. One day as I was desperately trying to dismantle some scaffolding on my own, the frame somehow fell and hit me on the head. I was so shocked I didn't know whether to laugh or cry, and didn't even know if I was hurt or not, I was in such a daze. When I came to my senses I frantically phoned Clive to tell him what had happened and asked him to phone me back in fifteen minutes to make sure I was o.k., as I really didn't know how badly I was hurt, or if I was concussed, I was so confused. I also had tremendous pain in my head where the scaffolding had hit me and of course a huge bump soon appeared. Luckily I didn't suffer any after effects, apart from the pain, and carried on working, though I was feeling very tearful and the fact that Clive didn't phone me back added to my despair. I felt so sorry for myself and the fact that Clive "didn't even care" added to my misery. When he finally came home that evening I was very cross with him for not bothering to phone me to check if I was o.k., He did explain that he hadn't had any phone signal all day, but it was just as well that I hadn't done myself any real damage!

Of course the bad weather of the autumn started to slow us down and we were still putting in the finishing touches an hour before the first guests arrived! My parents came to help on the day the first guests were due, and it was like the 'Sixty minute makeover' TV program, all of us rushing around, touching up paint, making beds, stealing ornaments from our own house to give it the finishing touches, it was totally mad. We were so pleased with the finished result though, and with its roof terrace patio, private Moroccan style courtyard and stunning mountain views from all of the windows, we were tempted to move in ourselves. What a relief to finally be finished, we could take a well earned rest. Little did we know quite how much time we would have to rest in the months to follow? The winter of 2008/2009 was the worst we could remember, and some say for thirty years. It felt like it rained every day, and if it wasn't raining it was snowing. We even had thick snow falling one evening and a thunder storm at the same time, very spooky!

One night we had hurricane force winds and woke up to find that the horse's field shelter had blown right over the fence and into the next paddock.

Our euphoria at finishing the new cottage was short lived. The recession was hitting hard. Clive had no building work at all, after nine years of never having to advertise and our holiday bookings had all but dried up, with people being too scared to book a holiday, and the British government advising taking holidays at home. We could not believe that after putting all the work and money into our second cottage, the holiday industry looked set to be devastated by the world wide financial crisis. Life became a constant battle to exist, with all the rescued animals to feed just adding to the burden. Each day was a struggle for survival, living on pasta, pancakes and soup made out of anything we could find. In hindsight, now that we have survived that trying time, we can at least be glad that it taught our children some very valuable lessons in life. They can all cook, making meals from the simplest ingredients and would never buy ready meals. They can also survive on very little money and are great at budgeting. They may not have enjoyed it at the time but I think they are proud of the way they can fend for themselves and do not yearn for material possessions in the way that most modern young people do. We are certainly very proud of them.

In some ways the lack of winter bookings was a miracle as it was so miserably wet, cold and muddy. The poor horses must have been bored out of their minds, and it was a daily battle to keep them fed, dry and warm. They certainly struggled to keep weight on. Of course it was miserable for all the animals. The cats and dogs just wanted to be in the house, complete with muddy paws of course. Sadly, just to add to our misery, poor little Phoebe, Elizabeth's ferret, at nearly nine years old had to be put to sleep. She had become so thin and had lost nearly all of her hair. She wasn't walking properly either, just stumbling around. She is sorely missed by all of us; she was such a little character. Even our fish caused us some concern for a while. We have a lovely Moroccan style water trough with goldfish in it. I couldn't believe my eyes one day when I walked into the courtyard and saw a huge heron sitting on the side of the trough helping himself to the fish. It was extremely annoying as we couldn't seem to scare him off, he must have been very hungry. He looked amazing, so handsome, but even so, we didn't want him to eat all our fish! We had to cover the water with wooden pallets for a few weeks until the heron gave up, not exactly attractive but needs must, and at least we didn't have guests in at the time.

The recession continued to hit harder and harder, we felt trapped in our terribly bleak life with no way out. With virtually no money coming in, we started to sell things, smaller things at first, such as a trailer, some tools to friends, anything to help put food on the table. People continually asked why we didn't sell the horses. They just couldn't understand that they were like my children and I would rather have them put to sleep than risk sending them on to another sad, cruel life. They had all lived in a herd for years now and I just couldn't do it to them, it would have haunted me for the rest of my life. In any case, horses had no value, as no one could afford to keep them and the papers were full of sad stories of neglect and abandonment, not to mention the thousands of horses going to slaughter because their owners could no longer afford to keep them. My sadness ate away at me; there was nothing to lift me out of the terrible feeling of desperation. I just didn't know how we were going to carry on. We became like hermits, with the weather so bad we just watched TV or went for walks, we lost touch with most of our friends as we couldn't afford to socialize; we certainly found out who our true friends were. Our last resort was to sell our beloved Land rover. A backward step in lots of ways, as without it Clive would not be able to do any building work if he did get any, but we had no choice, we literally needed money for food.

The worst worry of all was the thought of losing our beautiful home. Though we had bought it originally without a mortgage, we had since borrowed money to complete the renovations for the cottages, and we were getting deeper and deeper into arrears. The banks could offer no help, Spanish banks do not even allow overdrafts, they just kept telling us to pay any money in when we could, but as we didn't have any money that was a joke. We survived by the skin of our teeth, with bookings starting to creep in again, and Clive finding odd days work here and there. It is not an experience I ever want to repeat, but it proved to us that we could literally survive on nothing, and it is amazing what meals you can invent with the most limited ingredients. The only good thing to come out of it was our spur of the moment decision one day, when we were so miserable, cold and bored, to knock the wall down that divided the living room from the dining room. The house was arranged in such a way that it was impossible to position the sofas around the gorgeous inglenook fireplace, and we had had to resort to making the room with the fireplace our dining room, and putting our sofas in the adjoining room, which we then had to heat with a gas fire. As we had no money for gas, but plenty of firewood, we needed to find a solution in order to sit in front of the fire, and it suddenly occurred to us that we could knock the wall down. That was a life saver as it gave us something to do, that didn't cost money, as we already had the building materials we needed. It lifted our spirits for a while, and eventually also gave us a nice cosy living room, with sofas by the fire, after swapping the rooms around, a great idea born out of adversity – there is always something to be thankful for.

-Fourteen-

Guests behaving badly

It is bad enough coping with the weather ourselves when it is unseasonably bad, but having guests to worry about just adds to the misery. Even though we can do nothing about the weather, we feel so guilty when they arrive with children, expecting to swim in the heated pool and ride and walk and generally enjoy the countryside, and all they can do is huddle up in front of the wood burner with a DVD, or drive to the coast in the hope of slightly warmer temperatures. Even after all the years we never get over that feeling that we are responsible.

Obviously we want our guests to enjoy their holiday and we do our very best to make everything perfect for them. In recent years we have enjoyed guests from all over the world, with our use of Trip adviser to advertise broadening our market. Though we usually like our guests and often become good friends, occasionally they can irritate, you really do need to develop a thick skin to be in this line of business. Sometimes the little things that happen are amusing, such as our lovely Norwegian couple, in their sixties, who arrived with their parents, who were in their nineties. They had booked the El Establo cottage, which has one bedroom and the living room upstairs and the other bedroom and kitchen/ diner on the ground floor. For some reason they decided that it would be best for the parents to use the upstairs room, though the stairs are quite steep. Imagine our amazement when they knocked on the door and asked if Clive could put a bolt at the top of the stairs so that they could tie a rope (apparently the son was a sailor and knew his ropes!) and the elderly parents could pull themselves up and down the stairs! They did survive, with no broken bones but it was a worrying time for us to say the least. One of the most memorable guest episodes was with a young family staying in the El Granero cottage. They had already come across as slightly eccentric, with the odd little things they did, like laying all their washing out to dry on their patio floor instead of using the clothes airer, but nothing too extreme until this particular day. I was outside with the horses and Clive was upstairs in our house getting changed. When he came down into our kitchen he couldn't believe his eyes – the guest was frying an egg on our hob! Apparently the gas had run out on his cooker and as he couldn't find us, he just walked in to our kitchen and used our facilities to finish cooking his breakfast. Clive was so flabbergasted he didn't say anything. I found it incredible that someone could think nothing of invading our privacy like that, it was only an egg, we could have given him another one when we replaced the gas bottle. It was just as well that Clive didn't walk down into the kitchen naked!

The most annoying problems with guests are when they break things and don't say anything, but I suppose this is part of the business, we have to take the rough with the smooth. Not everyone is as respectful as we would hope, which isn't such a problem in the cottages, where the furniture is more user friendly, but when we had guests staying in our family farmhouse it used to break my heart, seeing people put wine glasses down on my polished oak furniture, when there were coasters provided, and on one occasion even carving a loaf of bread on my beautiful oak dining table.

One lovely German family did take the biscuit. They were great people, with three beautiful, polite, friendly children, but they allowed the children to run wild, picking all our fruit before it was ripe, making camps out of anything they could find, moving furniture about, even upsetting poor Pedro by moving all his straw bales about in his field and breaking the strings. The worst thing, the final straw, was when they piled all ten of our pool sun beds on top of each other to make a camp, with the metal dining chairs balanced on top of that. The first I knew of it was when I heard a tremendous clatter and went running to the pool area. The parents were all happily sitting on their patio, with no view of the pool area, while the children, the oldest being ten, were left to their own devises at the pool. When I got there the sun beds had all fallen down, tearing the cushions and chipping the paint on the metal chairs – I was so upset. To cap it all they had a big mixing bowl on the edge of the pool, full of a concoction of pistachios nuts, biscuits and water, a lovely mud pie, but not what we wanted in the pool! Oh dear, they were having such fun, it was just as well that the lovely elderly American guests in the other cottage had gone out for the day.

There have been lots of funny incidences over the years. As we often say, it takes all sorts, but on the whole our guests are lovely.

-Fifteen-

Another new arrival

A few years ago we found a stray new born lamb, who we named Minty (as in mint sauce). Clive jokes that we will eat him, but we all know he doesn't mean it – he loves Minty to bits, and Minty thinks that Clive is his Dad, following him everywhere. It was fate that brought them together really, as we were having problems with a lovely little dog that lived at the farm near us. Every time we rode the horses past he followed us home. As he was so small he could fit through the wire fencing so we couldn't deter him. He was so cute that it was tempting to keep him, as his owners just laughed when we took him back, and said we could have him. Anyway, we already had enough dogs, so much as we liked him, he had to go back. We were forever putting him in the car and driving him home, only to have him back again the next time we passed his farm. On one of the trips back with him, Clive had just dropped him off and was driving on when he saw something in his rear view mirror, running after the car. He at first thought that it was 'Little dog' again, but then noticed that it was a different colour so he stopped the car to investigate. Instead of a dog, it was a tiny new born lamb, hiding under the car. Clive picked him up and drove to all the nearby farms to ask if it was theirs, but nobody wanted to admit to owning him, so we had no choice but to bottle feed him. He was so pathetic and tiny, I have to admit that on his first night, we laid a big thick towel in the middle of our bed and let him sleep in with us, he was so lost and lonely. After that he slept in a box beside our bed. Clive had him on his side, as he had a tendency to get out of his box and run around the bedroom, his little hooves clop clopping on the terracotta tiles – not conducive to a good nights sleep. Clive's side of the bed was closer to the wall and we were able to fence him in with a wooden blanket box to make a little play pen. I did try to take a turn, but it felt strange sleeping on the wrong side of the bed (good excuse) so Clive ended up doing all the night feeds, waking every time he cried. Much as he hates to admit it, he was besotted with Minty, and even now that Minty is a full grown ram, and living with the goats, he lets him out to 'play' if he hears him crying. He is a lovely little character and follows me around when I am gardening, though I have to keep a close eye on him as he will eat everything. I did start putting a dog muzzle on him so that he could run around (he thinks he's a dog, and loves to run with them, putting in a skip and a jump every few strides) without wrecking the garden, but now that he is bigger he lives with the goats, and though they bullied him to start with, they get on very well now. I am sure that Minty thinks he is a goat though, as he is the first sheep I have seen that can climb on to the top of the goat house, he has obviously copied the goats and sits up there quite happily. Of course, we have now given ourselves another chore to add to our large list– sheep shearing, though luckily we have a friendly local farmer willing to come and shear him every summer, for the grand sum of three Euros. When we took the decision to put Minty in with the goats we had to get him castrated, as goats and sheep have different chromosomes, and if one of the goats was to get pregnant by Minty they would have a still born baby. Of course we also wanted Minty to stay a nice sweet sheep; we didn't want him to become an aggressive ram. Luckily at the time Lily was at Vet Nurse College in Malaga and was able to persuade her teacher that it would be a good idea to do the operation for the students to observe and help with. Lily can proudly say that she helped to castrate our sheep! When Minty was a couple of weeks old and started to live outside in the courtyard, Buster, our young dog had bonded with him so much that he also asked to sleep outside at night, and cuddled up next to Minty, as if he was protecting him. It was so sweet. We also still had 'Little dog', who had decided that he much preferred our farm to his, and a litter of three puppies that we had found abandoned in the olives. They all lived together in the courtyard and were such good friends. Thankfully, we gradually found homes for the puppies. The people that came to see the last puppy also fell in love with 'Little dog', as they could see that they were such good friends, and took him as well, so that was another problem solved, but poor Minty then just had Buster to play with. Tragically, on the very day that the last puppy and 'Little dog' were re-homed, Buster was accidently let out of the gates by the kids and got run over. Clive and I were in England when we heard the bad news.

Buster had run off and Elizabeth found him the following day, lying in a ditch with a broken leg. He was in a really bad way, as he could not put any weight on either back leg, and so had been unable to move, probably lying in the ditch in the cold all night. The kids got him to the vet, who said that he could either have an expensive operation to pin his leg together, be put to sleep or just be left to heal with a limp. He advised the third option, and being the other end of the phone we didn't know what to say, so we went along with the decision. When we arrived home, two days later, Buster looked so terrible that I was distraught that he hadn't been put to sleep. He was in a lot of pain and couldn't even get up to got to the toilet. Amazingly, within a couple of days, he was so much better, and able to move on his own. In hindsight, I was glad that I hadn't been here at the time of the accident as I think I would have been too emotional and would have made the wrong decision. Within a few months he could walk almost normally, it was hard to tell that he had ever broken the leg. When we first saw him after the accident, the leg just dangled pathetically and I thought that it would definitely have to be amputated, so it just goes to show how incredible the body is at healing itself. Buster still has the urge to escape if he can though, and will walk around pushing against the gates to see if they are locked properly. If he was with his mum Chici, and they happened to get out, they would be off running in the country side for hours, often coming back stinking of dead chickens. It was a constant problem as a lot of our guests didn't seem to feel the need to shut gates behind them, and very worrying, because as well as the threat of being run over, they could also have been shot by hunters. Chici was the ring leader, if Buster did get out on his own, he would just sniff around the car park and come back in, but with Chici the pair of them just ran and there was no hope of getting them back until they were ready. Sadly Chici recently died of leukemia. She was only about nine but at least she had had a happy life and we took the decision to have her put to sleep before she started to suffer. Poor Buster was lost for a while but he is fine now and Suzy makes a good replacement, she is always grooming him and playing rough and tumble, just as his mum used to. I hate to admit it but life is so much easier now, as if Buster gets out, he doesn't run off, it is quite a weight off my mind to be honest as it was so frustrating trying to get the guests to remember to close the gates. Scruffy doesn't tend to run off, but he does love to come out with the horses, running along side and darting off here and there to have a sniff at things. He is no trouble and I would take him with me all the time, but he does have a tendency to eat rotten dead things which does not have a good effect on his stomach! Suzy likes to get out and have a run, yapping her head off as she goes, but she never ventures far from home, being such a timid thing. With animals life will never be easy; there is always some little problem or other to tackle. I recently had another slightly traumatic occurrence with one of our hens. The poor thing had hopped up to have a drink out of the horse's water trough and fallen in. Luckily one of our guests raised the alarm, but by the time I got there the poor thing was almost completely submerged in the water, with only its eyes and beak visible. I plucked it out and wrapped it in towels, rubbing it continuously to try to warm it. Every time the towel became too wet I wrapped it in another straight from the tumble drier to try to get it warm. Its body temperature had fallen so low that it felt like it was an oven ready chicken straight from the fridge. The pathetic little thing remained very calm and let me work on it for a couple of hours, until finally it felt warm and dry and was able to walk around.

Incredibly it was fine, with nothing to show for its ordeal. I was totally amazed as I really thought that it would die. I just hope that it doesn't happen again, as there is no way that I can stop the chickens drinking from the trough if that's what they want to do, they will even drink at the same time as the horses, they are totally fearless. I have had to put some big stones in now, just in case.

We have had the horses 'bare hoofed' for about two years now. It has proved to be incredibly successful, and a bonus in so many ways. Their feet are stronger and healthier than they have ever been, with absolutely no cracks, or any problems at all, whatever the weather or terrain. They are all completely sound, even those that are ridden a lot, and are as sure footed as mountain goats to ride, which is lovely. To start with we had some special boots for

Hercules, as being an English Cob, his feet were not as good as the Spanish horses. Now though, if anything, he has the best feet, and they are certainly better than they ever were when he had shoes on, despite the fact that he is one of our most popular, and therefore most regularly ridden horses. It is so lovely to be able to do their feet ourselves, without the trauma of a farrier's visit. It's especially good for young horses, who will never have to suffer the bad treatment that some of the old horses have had to put up with in their lives. I have had a couple of good farriers in the past, but there are some that will hit the horse with whatever tool they have in their hand if they don't behave. The young horses have such perfect feet, and now they will never have to have them spoilt by having nails banged into them. We are very lucky that the horses live in the perfect environment for being bare foot. It is important to have a varied terrain, with different surfaces for them to walk on, and with their compacted mud paddock, with stones regularly working their way to the surface and the concrete areas around the open stables, it couldn't be better. It also helps that we regularly ride most of the horses through the stream at the bottom of the field, as a foot bath is also a bonus, and of course the ridden horses encounter a wide variety of terrain when out riding, from stony tracks to stubble fields, soft olive groves and the occasional quiet tarmac road.

Our first two youngsters, Bonny and Leo have proved to be two of our most popular horses for our riding clients. It is so rewarding, as we have had them from foals and we can take pride in the fact that they are the product of our making. Lily did most of the work when they were first backed and ridden, with John taking on Leo to continue his training. They have been a delight from the beginning, and we now have the privilege of riding Leos' other offspring – Fern, Picasso and Spirit, and of course Twiggy who is also Bonny's foal.

-Sixteen-

Helper horrors

Our life seems guaranteed not to run smoothly and the spring of 2010 was no exception. We are certainly not alone in having our travel plans disrupted by the volcano eruption in Iceland, but the extent we had to go to, to even try to achieve the holiday in the first place probably takes some beating.

With fifteen horses, four dogs, seven cats, two goats, one sheep, chickens and fish, not to mention the guests , pool and garden, a holiday is almost impossible at the best of times, which is why in the twelve years we have lived here we haven't managed more than a couple of short holidays to visit friends and family. That spring however, after the stresses and worry of the recession, we were determined that we would have a well earned break. At Christmas some friends of ours told us about a website www.helpx .net, which links hosts with helpers, the idea being that as a host you get free help in exchange for bed and board, and as a helper you get a free holiday in exchange for a few hours work a day. It sounded brilliant, and indeed the young lad from Australia that our friends had staying was a great recommendation. We duly signed up for it and soon had lots of requests from people wanting to come and help us. You can specify your requirements, so in our case it was horse experience, but even so, we received lots of enquiries from people who saw it as a good opportunity to have a holiday with riding and heated pool on tap, and couldn't even ride a horse! The e-mails along the lines of 'I have always wanted to learn to ride' were politely declined, but some of the replies seemed very promising and we arranged for a few girls to come and help out. Our idea was that we would have a couple of helpers for a longer term, i.e. a couple of months, so that they had time to get to know the ropes, in order for us to then feel safe in leaving them to hold the fort for a few days while we took a trip to see Lily in Germany and John and family in the UK.

The first girl to arrive was really lovely, but unfortunately, though she had originally planned to stay a couple of months, she had been invited to join her boyfriend in Japan, and of course that was an offer too good to refuse. Not to worry , we thought, there was still the other girl, and we had also asked our local young friend , Coral, to come and help while we were away too, along with our other son Harry, who very kindly agreed to use some of his annual holiday to come home and cover for us. All the best laid plans as they say.... We set off for the airport to collect the second girl, having carefully checked her email for her arrival time and flight details. After waiting at the airport for over an hour and watching the last straggling passengers from her flight leaving, we realised that she was not on the flight and had no alternative but to go home. Eventually, later that night, I received an email from her, explaining that she had been taken unwell at Madrid airport after flying in from Greece, and had missed the flight. She informed us that she was going to get a train to Malaga, so the next day we set off again to collect her from the train station. We arrived to find a little waif and stray sitting on her suitcase, looking like a gust of wind would blow her over, and very pale and unhealthy looking. Oh well, she seemed nice enough, and explained that she had fainted and was not allowed to board the plane, and luckily a flight attendant had taken pity on her and allowed her to sleep at her house until she could catch the train the next day. On her first morning she failed to get up in time to help, and then admitted that she felt too ill to work and had a chest infection. She also admitted to being allergic to cats, and having asthma! Not a good combination in a household with so many pets. Had she been honest before she came we would never have agreed to her coming to help. Of course I felt sorry for her and told her to stay in bed, taking her food and making a fuss of her, she looked such a lost little sole. Once she felt a bit better she was able to help with the horses and was not a bad rider, quite fearless and willing to ride the younger horses, but with no common sense – if she needed to go from one side of a horse to the other she would walk underneath them! She was only about five foot tall but even so! She could not be trusted around the horses, we always had to watch her and check up on what she was doing, as she would leave pitch forks in stables or forget to shut gates. The trouble was, she was such a pathetic little thing that it was hard to be cross with her, and like a fool I tolerated her behaviour. Something else that had us worried though was her eating habits. As I said, she was a tiny little thing, but she could eat like a horse. I quickly learned not to put food in serving bowls for everyone to help themselves, as she would literally finish off everything, and she could knock back a large glass of red wine in one go. I just thought that she had a good appetite, until the day that we had to go out and leave her to get her own lunch. I had made a huge pot of lentil stew, big enough to feed a family for two days, and left it on the hob. I had also left a loaf of bread out for her to help herself, but because I had started to notice food going missing, I had also hidden one inside a tin in a cupboard. When we returned from our day out I was horrified to discover that she had eaten all of the stew, the loaf that I had left out for her, and she had also found the hidden loaf and eaten that. I was so upset, I knew that I needed to talk to her about it but didn't know how to. It was the arrival of other helpers that brought it to a head, as they admitted that they had caught her being sick after meals, and of course I couldn't allow her to eat all the food, leaving nothing for the other girls. The final straw was when she collapsed on the floor in the helper's apartment. The two girls sharing with her came knocking on the door after we had gone to bed, in a terrible state, saying that she was unconscious and they didn't know what to do. I couldn't wake her, and looked through her bag to see if there was any sign of medicine or drugs she may have taken. To my horror I discovered empty packets of food, even frozen food, that she had stolen from us, it was very sad. There was no sign of anything she could have taken though, and we all decided that it was the combination of her asthma treatment and alcohol and left her to sleep it off. The next day I contacted her dad who confirmed that she had suffered from Bulimia for years. I had to ask her to go, after helping her find somewhere else to move on to. Unfortunately she refused to go home, though it would have been the best thing for her. Undeterred, we put an emergency advert on the Helpx site asking for cover for the holiday, and soon had a phone call from a girl who was working in Seville and could come and stay for the required dates. She sounded great, though she did explain that she had recently split up from her long term boyfriend, which set off a few warning bells, but we arranged to collect her from Malaga train station and thought things were finally settled. Unbelievably, bad luck struck again, as within a few days of her arrival, she asked if her boyfriend could come to stay and work for us as well, as they were now back together. Slightly apprehensive, but determined not to give up, we agreed that he could, and for a few days it was fine, with Clive getting some much needed help with maintenance around the farm, but it was not to last, as one night they borrowed our bikes, cycled to the nearest bar, and while trying to cycle back drunk in the early hours they both managed to come off the bikes and get run over in the process. We knew nothing about it until they surfaced the next afternoon (we had wondered why they hadn't got up to help us in the morning!) Needless to say, we couldn't trust them to be here while we were away, so we were back to having just Harry and Coral again.

All this worry had taken its toll, and Clive and I were now even more desperate for a few days away. I set about writing the mile long list of things to do for Harry and Coral, started thinking about packing and allowed myself to get excited – we were actually going to have a holiday after two years without a break. The flights and hotels were booked, the arrangements were made with friends and family in the UK, we were all set. Then of course disaster struck again in the form of an erupting volcano. We watched the news , frantically hoping that it would all be sorted out by the time we were due to travel, surely after all this worry and effort we would get our holiday? No such luck – our flights were cancelled, and for us there wasn't even the consolation of having a holiday another time – this break took far too much planning, and Harry had used up his holiday for nothing, so that was it, we had lost our only chance. Dreadfully disappointed we accepted the fact that we wouldn't be going anywhere.

There was another problem though, we had two more Helpx girls staying, who had been with us for their two week college break, and they were now stranded with no way of getting home. There was only one thing for it – mad as it was, we decided that we would drive to the UK, dropping the girls off with their mum in Dover on the way, and salvage the second part of our holiday. This wasn't quite as easy as it sounds though. As bad luck would have it, the new Land rover that we had recently purchased proved to have problems starting and we had taken it back to the garage we bought it from – a two and a half hour drive away. We were still waiting for them to tell us if it was ready to collect and because it had had to go back so soon after we had bought it, we also still had four new tyres waiting at the local tyre fitters, ready to put on. Our spur of the moment decision to drive to the UK couldn't have been more complicated. We waited with baited breath for the phone call to say that the Land rover was ready for collection, and finally, on the morning of the day that we needed to leave, it was ready. Clive set off with Harry to collect the car, calling in at the tyre people on the way to beg them to fit the tyres as soon as they got back. After a five hour return journey the Land rover was left to have its new tyres fitted while Clive frantically arrived home to finish his packing and at four o'clock we set off at last, only stopping for diesel, snacks and a two hour sleep in a motorway service station. Clive loves driving and never gets tired. Bearing in mind the amount of driving he had already done before we set off, that was just as well! Thankfully, in our rush to get away we did find time to quickly book the ferry online, as when we arrived at Calais there were thousands of people queuing to try to buy tickets, having caught coaches or hired cars, in a desperate attempt to get home. It was a terrible sight, all those poor tired people, many with young children, it made us aware that though we had been through a tough few days, things could have been worse!

We were very sad at not being able to see Lily in Hamburg, but we were able to see John and our granddaughter Myah and enjoy some lovely times with all our friends and family, so though we only had three whole days there, with two days driving either side, with only a couple of hours sleep in the car , it was an adventure, (albeit a very expensive one!) and when we arrived back home Harry and Coral had done such a great job, we did wonder why we had even bothered to try to find extra help in the first place.

The next spring we were slightly dubious about having more helpers, with the problems we had experienced, but the idea is a good one in principle, and we decided to give it another go, as we desperately needed some help to ride the younger horses ready for the summer. Having enjoyed the help of our Slovakian helper Jana the previous summer, we took the chance on Pavlina, from the Czech Republic, as from her profile she looked like she would be very similar in character. She was travelling with her English boyfriend James, and the two of them made a great team. They achieved amazing results with the horses, worked hard and used their initiative – it was great to have them around and they stayed for four months, getting on well with our guests and enjoying the paella nights and three course meals we often had to provide for the full board clients – it was a mutually rewarding experience and we would have them back to stay any time. Pavlina , like Lily, is very into natural horsemanship and it was a joy to watch her with the horses, she genuinely loved working with them.

Luckily for us, just two weeks after they left, Lily came home for three months and we were able to carry on the good work. It was lovely to have Lily back home to ride with again, and to see that she still had all her skills with the horses. By the end of the summer we were riding all of the horses out on hacks in just rope head collars, and even Polly, who has always been a bit crazy, was now behaving like a calm old plodder. Incredible to think that by just putting a rope head collar on her, instead of a traditional bridle with bit, it somehow changed her character and instead of wanting to run , she is now so relaxed.

I would have loved to have had Lily home for longer, but she has now started another exciting chapter in her young life – teaching scuba diving in Mexico. Soon after qualifying she saw a teaching vacancy for someone who could speak fluent German, English and Spanish. Her first job application and she got it! We are so pleased for her and very proud of her independence and determination to do what she wants to do.

-Seventeen-

A donkey to add to the menagerie?

I know that I should think myself very lucky to have fifteen horses, especially as I had wanted a horse of my own since I was a small child. However, I do have to admit to not having fulfilled another of my yearnings – to have a donkey. They are such adorable creatures, I could easily be tempted, but even I know that I have to draw the line. We have quite enough animals as it is and I think that a donkey would be a step too far for Clive, however tolerant he has been with me up until now.

I did almost gain a couple of donkeys by accident a few years ago though! One of our riding routes takes us past a field with donkeys in it. Unfortunately, unknown to me, on this particular day part of the fence had been trampled down. My heart sank as we approached the field and I saw the donkey running towards its escape route, followed by its very cute little foal. With a family of two adults and two children, all beginners, to consider, I could hardly think about trying to out run it. As the donkey got closer I could feel my horse tensing up. Of course, just to make it worse, the donkey then started braying at the top of its voice. Donkeys are not a horse's favourite thing at the best of times, but to have one so close and making such an awful noise must have been its worst nightmare. Thankfully my horses are very well behaved and don't spook easily.

I could tell that they weren't happy, but they didn't do anything about it. I had to decide what to do very quickly, before anything happened. I jumped off of my horse, Hercules, who bless him, just stood there while I chased the donkeys back into a neighbouring field. As they ran down the field I was able to quickly walk all the horses on past the opening. Thankfully, by the time they came running back up the field, they decided to turn the opposite way to us, back to their friends, and we were able to get away. Another time, about a month later, when I thought the fence had been mended, I wasn't quite so lucky. I was taking an Australian tourist out on a hack and decided to take the route again. I had just been thinking to myself that I would ask him if he wanted to try a short trot, when trotting up behind us came another donkey. I just had time to shout 'can you trot?' and with his nod we were off. Unfortunately this didn't work, and as I thought I might be pushing my companion too much to suggest a canter we came back to walk, with the donkey still following. As before, I jumped off of my horse, Lucy, who was getting a bit fed up with having a donkey on her tail, and turned round to try to shoo the donkey away. It then became like a scene from the children's game 'what's the time mister wolf?' Every time I turned around, the donkey stopped and looked away, then as soon as I started walking again; it started to creep up behind us. It was hysterical. In the end I decided to phone John, who came out in the car with a lead rope, to try to get the donkey back to where it had come from. By now we were getting closer to home and I was beginning to think that I would have yet another rescue animal on my hands. John kept scaring the donkey back, but it just kept following. We came to a goat farm where I explained to the farmer what had happened. He thought it was really funny and said that there would be another donkey loose in the campo, as if it was an every day occurrence. At this point the donkey decided to go and visit the farmer's horse, tethered up on the hillside and we were able to make our escape. My Australian client thoroughly enjoyed our adventure, and it certainly gave him something to talk about to his friends afterwards.

Harry had a similar run in with a stray stallion, which could have had a much more serious outcome. In Spain it is quite normal to see horses left loose in the countryside, with their front legs tied together, or hobbled, as it is known. It is a very distressing sight for me at the best of times, and I have witnessed numerous poor horses lumbering around with the awful, awkward gait that is produced by this horrible act. It usually works quite well for the owners as a form of confinement; most horses do not wander far when tied in this way. The other method used to keep horses in open fields is to tie them on a long rope, which not only is upsetting to see, in the heat of the summer, when the horse has no shade or water, and cannot even touch another horse to groom and socialise, but also has potentially dangerous side effects. Sometimes the horse gets excited when we are passing by and gets itself into a tangle, but worse than that is when a mare is tied, with her foal loose. This works ok for a young foal, but once they start to get braver, they follow us when we are passing on the horses and the poor mother becomes so stressed, desperately throwing herself to the end of her rope, trying to follow the foal. Fortunately, on the few times this has happened, the foal has always given up after short distance and run back to Mum, but it is very worrying at the time.

Anyway, Harry was taking two young women guests for a long country hack. They were both good riders and they were enjoying lots of canters and taking in the scenery, with Harry having an equally good time being their guide and showing off his considerable riding skills. On route they passed a field with a stallion in but didn't think any more of it until they were cantering up another track and suddenly saw the stallion galloping towards them, across fields, with his front legs tied together. Harry said it was an amazing site, because of the strange movement of the horse, it looked like something out of a horror film, it was really quite disturbing. The horse soon caught up with them and as one of our horses, Lucy, was in season, and consequently of considerable interest to the stallion, Harry decided to jump off of his horse and try to scare it away. Unfortunately this didn't work and the situation was getting very worrying. The only other thing Harry could think of to try was out running the by now very hyped up stallion. He quickly vaulted on to his horse, Capri and shouted to the girls to go. Fortunately they were able to eventually out run the beast, and the girls arrived back at the farm with a very exciting story to tell their parents!

-Eighteen-

The future looks bright

Life on the farm has certainly been full of ups and downs, and has never been easy. Being self employed in these difficult times, it will be a while before we can feel financially secure, and we still have moments when we are living on egg and chips, praying for the next booking to come in. Things have started to pick up for us finally though , with all three of our guest accommodations being booked for most of the year, and Clive even has some building work again. It will take time to get completely back on our feet and feel comfortable, but life has been easier for us this year and we have been able to pay our bills, which is something we are very thankful for, having been through the recession. Clive even had some building work from Pedro, which was a first, as he has never worked for Spanish before; they tend to be very loyal to their own builders. Clive was actually working along side the Spanish builder that Pedro always uses, and he really enjoyed it, having the chance to practice his Spanish for a while, though he had to bite his tongue every time Miguel told him how to do something, despite Clive being the more skilled builder of the two. Luckily Clive is very easy going and tolerant, though he did get a bit fed up with having to lend all his tools, something he has got used to over the years, as it seems that every time Pedro employs a builder or painter, they come knocking on our door to borrow trowels, ladders, all sorts of things that you would think they would have themselves, it is quite funny really, and we don't really mind, it is nice that they feel they can ask, and makes us feel that we are accepted as part of the community.

The horses were great this year too, the riding was just perfect and I am very proud of what we have achieved, after all the years of hard work.

Another lovely and unexpected bonus we have found over the last couple of years is having guests arrive to stay in the two cottages, never having met before, but soon becoming friends. The cottages both have their own private patios and we have found that our guests mostly keep to their own areas, and seem to have the pool to themselves too, as one family tends to be out sight seeing while the other has a day at the pool and visa versa, but for some reason we have noticed over the last couple of summers that some guests get on so well, it has often felt like they have known each other for years. It is especially nice if guests have children of similar ages. One year we had guests in both cottages from Denmark. They booked separately and arrived, not even knowing that the other cottage would have a family from their country staying in it. Imagine their surprise to find that not only were they from the same country, but they were from the same town and one of the Mums taught at the other family's daughter's school! Their two daughters were exactly the same age, even sharing a birthday, and both loved horses – what a coincidence!

A lot of holiday makers these days like to check out their destination on Tripadviser. This has proved to be a real asset to us, we now have many wonderful reviews from happy guests and of course this also helps us to encourage more bookings, from all over the world. We have even had the honour this year of being given two awards from Tripadviser for 'Top vacation rental' and ' Rated excellent' – these emblems are certainly an asset to our website and we are so proud that all our hard work has paid off. Though it is extra work for us we do offer evening meals for guests, if booked in advance. This is something that we have been doing for a few years now for our full board riding holiday guests, but we have found that a lot of holidaymakers in our self catering cottages like the convenience of having a meal on site, without the worry of drinking and driving. Our most popular meal is our Paella night, (though I do most of the cooking, this is Clive's speciality) when we cook a huge, authentic paella and everyone eats together at the big wooden table in the outer, communal courtyard. It makes such an enjoyable, sociable evening, all sitting around chatting, with the crickets chirping in the background and the stars twinkling overhead, often rounded off with the children all jumping in the pool for a midnight swim. The guests love it and it makes us feel very happy to be providing this extra service.

A lovely memory to hold on to, as winter fast approaches and we wonder what new challenges the year ahead will throw at us. Will the threat of another world wide recession send us plunging back into austerity, or will we carry on growing from strength to strength - we can only wait and see.

Printed in Great Britain
by Amazon

78845990R00088